KILKENNYCOOKBOOK

Recipes from the Kilkenny Kitchen

Contributors:

Recipes by Catherine Curran, Claire Russell,
Annemarie Conway.

Foreword by John Rocha

Text by David Pritchard

Recipes edited by Catherine Curran and Claire Russell

Book and Jacket design by Brian Murphy

Photography by Hugh Glynn

Published by Real Ireland Design.
27 Beechwood Close, Boghall Rd., Bray, Co. Wicklow, Ireland.
Tel + 353 1 2860799 Fax + 353 1 2829962
e-mail info@realireland.ie
web www.realireland.ie

A CIP catalogue record for this book is available from the
British Library.

ISBN 0946887-14-4

'Our parents, the late Christy and Maureen Kelleher
were our first and greatest role models.
We dedicate this cookbook to their memory with profound
gratitude for their inspiration and example.'

Marian O'Gorman and Bernadette Kelleher-Nolan
Directors of the Kilkenny Group

Contents

John Rocha

Born in Hong Kong and of Chinese and Portuguese decent John moved to London to study fashion and finally settled in Ireland during the 1980's.

In 1994 John was British Designer of the Year. Through this time John has developed his own distinctive style, constantly working with new fabrics and techniques.

In 1997 he launched 'John Rocha at Waterford Crystal' a range of contemporary crystal that continues to develop and now includes a collection of coloured crystal vessels.

More recently John has moved into interiors, collaborating in the design of the Morrison Hotel in Dublin, as well as residential and commercial projects in Ireland, the UK and Budapest.

In 2002 John Rocha launched a collection of organic shaped contemporary jewellery.

John Rocha was awarded a CBE in the Queen's Jubilee New Year's honours list in 2002 for his contribution to the fashion industry.

Foreword

I believe that food is such a simple yet a very personal and social pleasure. It has the potential to give us intimate moments alone, as well as with each other. It brings us together and acts as a reflection of our cultural, economic and social values.

Our cultural growth, social diversity as well as dynamic economic expansion find expression in the type of produce we use and how we use it and consume it. To this end, cookbooks are windows into a world of new flavours, new tastes, new experiences.

Today's Ireland is one of growth and expansion; the Diaspora returning with a variety of multicultural influences to delight and enhance the Irish palette. Our strong economy and closer ties with the world have brought many new culinary traditions from distant lands, their cultures and new experiences of exotic flavours. My love of Ireland combined with my diverse cultural background also inspires me to blend the influences and richness of other cultures in my work.

I am delighted to have the opportunity to introduce the Kilkenny Cookbook. Kilkenny has always provided a representation of craft, design and a modern sense of Ireland that retains the important qualities of Irish culture. This cookbook follows that philosophy in representing the food of the Kilkenny Restaurant; successfully combining new flavours with the richness of local earthy produce and traditions, reminding us how Irish values can meld with new influences.

Contemporary busy lifestyles invite the need for cookbooks like this one that ground us to our roots as well as take us forward to a New Ireland, and give us a warm belly!

John Rocha

The Kilkenny Kitchen is a winner of the
'Denny Breakfast Award' in association with
Georgina Campbell.

'Dublin City winner 2003'.

KILKENNY

RECIPES

Soups and Chowders

Soups and Chowders

Salads and Dressings

Salads and Dressings

RECIPES (cont.)

Salads and Dressings

Vegetable Dishes

R E C I P E S (cont.)

Meat Dishes

Meat Dishes

64

76

Fish Dishes

Fish Dishes

6

R E C I P E S (cont.)

RECIPES (cont.)

Bakery

Bakery (cont.)

Desserts

Desserts

100

118

The History of Kilkenny

To anyone who works in a restaurant or, indeed, cooks at home for guests, the greatest compliment always comes when the diner requests a copy of the recipe. At Kilkenny these requests come daily and have done since we first opened our restaurant overlooking Trinity College at our flagship shop in Nassau Street in 1976. So now, nearly thirty years later, we have finally come up with the goods.

A long time coming, you might say, but we think you'll agree, well worth the wait!

KILKENNY - Forty years of design excellence.

In 1961, the Irish Export Board invited five eminent Scandinavian experts to investigate the state of design in the country. Their report, although critical of the low levels of design awareness, held good news, suggesting that Ireland had a unique opportunity, denied by circumstances to many more developed countries, of making a great contribution, not alone to her own prosperity and culture, but to the culture of Western Europe.

It was this comment that encouraged the Irish government to set up the Kilkenny Design Workshop, its brief being to develop the crafts industry and to promote better design. Beautifully situated in the eighteenth century stables

Kilkenny Restaurant - Nassau Street

Kilkenny Counter - Nassau St.   Céire

opposite Kilkenny Castle, it was opened in April 1963 by the then government minister Patrick Hillery and quickly became a valuable training ground and platform for Irish craftspeople working in many mediums, playing a vital role in raising industrial design standards. In 1965, a small shop and exhibition area was opened at the front of the Kilkenny Design Workshop premises.

Originally intended only for the display of products by the craftspeople working there, it soon began selling pieces from other Irish designers as well.

And so Kilkenny – and its philosophy to offer customers a modern and contemporary interpretation based on the very best in Irish traditions – was born.

By 1976, demand for this unique product offering had grown sufficiently to warrant the opening of a custom-built 'retail exhibition centre' in Nassau Street Dublin that was to become the country's premiere showcase for contemporary

Catherine and Claire

Irish craft and design. In addition it featured a superb restaurant offering top quality home made Irish food. At 1,500 square metres, it offered almost twice as much retail space as its counterpart in Kilkenny City and the spacious and uncluttered layout allowed a far more open approach to display than was common at the time. The range of merchandise available reflected a renaissance in Irish craft and design, eventually growing to include clothing, accessories, jewellery, glass, ceramics, table and kitchenware, books, stationery, textiles, furnishings and lighting which featured the work of over 130 individuals by 1982.

As the 1980s progressed, and innovative designers like John Rocha emerged, Irish products began to be internationally fashionable. The Design Centre thrived, and provided a staging point where merchandise by our craftspeople could be introduced to the widest possible market.

In 1988, the Irish government sold the Kilkenny Design Centre, Nassau Street to Blarney Woollen Mills, a Cork retail company owned by the Kelleher family who took the decision to retain its unique ethos and craft-based identity and remain faithful to the principle that it should showcase high quality crafts from Irish designers.

One of the kitchen team

In July 1999, the store became simply Kilkenny, an independent entity, under the ownership of Marian O'Gorman. Under her guidance the Nassau Street shop continues to flourish, whilst new Kilkenny shops have been opened in Galway and Killarney.

KILKENNY TODAY

The name Kilkenny continues to be synonymous with the finest Irish craftsmanship, but contemporary tastes are far more sophisticated than they once were, and the constant demand for new and better products has encouraged the Group to become more flexible and imaginative in its approach to retailing. Whilst retaining its individual suppliers, Kilkenny has also introduced several own-brand ranges, for instance the 'Art of Dressing' ladies fashion label and 'Passionate about Taste' foods, which are designed in-house. In addition, leading designers in the various craft disciplines are regularly commissioned to make exclusive products that are sold only in Kilkenny.

Kilkenny Restaurant - Nassau St.

Counter Service - Nassau St.   *Making Coffee - Nassau St.*   *Some of the team*

Many of Kilkenny's suppliers, such as Louis Mulcahy and Stephen Pearce, have been internationally recognised as masters of their art. Irish glass has also made its name abroad, with companies like Jerpoint and Tipperary emerging alongside the long established Waterford Crystal. Interestingly, Waterford subsequently commissioned leading designer John Rocha to create a contemporary range – a move which has proven most successful for them. The photographs accompanying the recipes in this cookbook testify to the skills of the Irish craftspeople working in these areas. Kilkenny stocks the exquisite ceramics, table settings and glassware featured in them.

The years since the opening of the Kilkenny Design Workshops have seen Irish craft and design evolve into a booming domestic and export industry. But its ongoing success still depends on the nurturing of new talent and products. As it faces into the future, Kilkenny is proud to be a part of this process.

Trinity College - Dublin.

AND SO - TO THE FOOD

When our flagship store was opened in 1976, it featured a Café and Restaurant offering wholesome meals and patisseries, located on the first floor and offering pleasant views into the grounds of Trinity College. At first it offered a welcome respite for the busy shopper after the visual and sensory experiences of the shopfloor below. But soon, thanks to the excellence of the food, our restaurant became a draw in itself. For many people it has become an obvious meeting place – the south-side equivalent of Clery's Clock. A must for visiting coach parties. A favourite amongst locals and tourists alike for its incomparable Irish Stew. Its homemade breads and soups. Paninis, salads and sandwiches that make a meal in themselves. And, naturally, nothing but the best in coffee and cakes. All made from the finest of ingredients, sourced from the cream of Irish suppliers.

The success of the Café and Restaurant in Dublin has been such that food has become an important part of the Kilkenny Brand which is now as strongly associated with the quality and reputation of its restaurant as with the designer crafts featured on the shopfloor.

"The array of fresh homemade food brings on unattractive attacks of indecision and weak will." Food and Wine Magazine

Just as the designers are at the heart of the success of our shops, it is the people behind the scenes at our restaurants and cafes that make them so popular.

KILKENNY Café and Restaurant - Dublin

Catherine Curran
Manager, Kilkenny Restaurant, Dublin.
Educated at Cathal Brugha St. Catering College with practical training in the E.S.B. Head Office Dining Club and experience in all sorts of establishments from a Kosher Restaurant to running her own sandwich delivery business in Covent Garden, finally led Catherine to the position of Restaurant Manager, Kilkenny Nassau St.

'What can I say except that it's an absolute pleasure to work here with a team who are amongst the most hardworking and dedicated that I have ever come across. People like Dolores Harold who has been here for 12 years and keeps a watchful eye on our hygiene standards. Every morning each member of the counter staff are briefed by the kitchen chefs on the ingredients of the day's salads, soups and hot meals.

Catherine Curran

Of course, our customers are terrific too. I think the fact that they enjoy it so much comes across very clearly. At lunchtimes particularly you'll find a great atmosphere, with everyone prepared to share a table or make room for someone. Often it's all hands on deck just to keep the queue moving and make sure all our customers get the service they deserve. Fortunately, we have staff who are fluent in French, Italian, German, and Japanese, amongst others, at hand to answer visitor's queries.

Because of its position in the heart of Dublin, the restaurant also has a really interesting clientéle. Over the years we have had many famous people in the café – for instance Brad Pitt, Jeremy Irons, Billy Connolly and Eric Clapton. Also our regulars include many leading Irish politicians, along with academics and students from Trinity College, which is just across the road from us. And they all appreciate the fact that we only use suppliers who provide the highest quality produce, one of the reasons for us winning the Georgina Campbell 'Best Breakfast Award for Dublin 2003'.

"Kilkenny seeks to offer the 'Best of Irish' in terms of crafts, clothing, merchandise – and particularly food, and its continuing popularity is evidence that it is indeed succeeding."
Hotel and Catering Review

Annemarie Conway

Claire Russell

But the real key to the café's popularity must be our wonderful chefs, without whom none of this would be possible. Like our Head Chef, Cordon Bleu trained Claire Russell who has been a member of the Kilkenny Restaurant team for the last five years. She reflects the modern multicultural Ireland, having lived and worked in Spain, Morocco, South Africa and France. And Anne marie Conway who has become an outstanding Chef having started with Kilkenny at the tender age of seventeen.

Together they wish you the best of luck with the recipes in this book and the advicethey offer is 'Don't be afraid to try!'

GLUTEN-FREE RECIPES

One of the notable aspects of the menus at Kilkenny– and, indeed of this Cookbook - is the inclusion of a wide selection of gluten-free foods. This is a godsend for the many Irish people who have a coeliac condition, as not all restaurants c ater for their specific needs. So the chefs set to work, beginning by including one or two suitable dishes on their daily menu to test the response. Hugely appreciated by customers, gluten-free options are now a regular feature and range from cakes and scones to main dishes and soups, opening up the delights of previously forbidden food to many people every day.

Keeping gluten-free food separate in the kitchen

PASSIONATE ABOUT TASTE - Speciality Food Range -

In 2002, some of the Kilkenny Team, along with other food professionals, were involved in tasting and choosing 'Passionate About Taste' - Kilkenny's new specialty delicatessen range. The final selection marked the culmination of months of research, since the company was determined to source the finest products available.

Kilkenny planned to capture the quality of good homemade cooking, and they wanted traditional recipes and natural ingredients for the Irish-made foods, oils, preserves and confectionery. Launched in September 2002, it has since become a firm favourite with customers. Along with tasty treats like waffles, hand - made chocolates, and preserves, there are award winning relishes and chutneys, and like everything else in Kilkenny it is constantly evolving in line with contemporary flavours and trends.

Passionate About Taste - selection of the speciality food range

Kilkenny Galway

Kilkenny French Onion Soup

This famous French soup is warming and comforting in winter. It is simple to make, can be reheated when needed and is suitable for vegetarians if made with vegetable stock. The large amount of onions is the secret of good French onion soup.

Serves 6

Ingredients

2kg / 4lbs / 16Cups Onions sliced

125g / 4oz / $^1/_2$Cup Butter

3 Garlic cloves, crushed

30g / 2tb / 2T Flour

Salt and pepper

275ml / 10floz / 11/4Cups White wine or dry vermouth

1.7L / 3pts / 6Cups Beef stock

1tsp / 1t Sugar (helps the onions to brown)

2 Baguettes for croûtes

12 Thin slices of gouda cheese

CHEF'S TIP

This soup can be prepared ahead, cook using a heavy bottomed pot and refrigerate for up to 2 days. It can also be frozen. Cool quickly, pack & freeze.

Method

The onions for this soup need a long, slow cooking in butter and a slow simmering in stock to develop the deep, rich flavour and colour.

Allow 2 hours from start to finish.

Cook onions slowly in butter, raise temperature and stir in salt and sugar.

Cook for 30 mins stirring frequently until the onions have turned a deep golden brown.

Sprinkle in flour and stir for 1 min.

Off the heat, blend in the boiling stock.

Add the wine and season to taste.

Simmer partially covered for 40 mins., stirring occasionally.

To Prepare Croûtes

Cut bread into 12 slices and toast on both sides under grill.

Spread one side of each croûte with gouda.

Pour soup into tureen or soup dishes .

Float the croûtes on top and brown under a hot grill.

 Nutritional Advice: Garlic and onions offer enormous health benefits, both are associated with the prevention of heart disease.

Suggested Wine: Sauvignon Blanc.

Kilkenny French Onion Soup

Creamy Asparagus Soup

Asparagus soup should be pale green in colour and creamy in texture. It is traditionally served at Christmas time.

Serves 6

Ingredients

2lbs / 30-40 Spears of asparagus.
1 med Onion
50g / 2oz / $\frac{1}{4}$Cup Butter
50g / 2oz / $\frac{1}{2}$Cup Plain flour
1.2L / 2pt / 5Cups Milk
250ml / 8floz / 1Cup Cream
Salt and pepper
2 Egg yolks

Method

CHEF'S TIP

It is important not to overcook this soup as it quickly loses it's delicate flavour.

Cut Asparagus into small pieces, finely dice the onion.

Melt the butter in a saucepan, add onion and asparagus and cook for 6 mins.

Draw aside, add the flour and cook for 1 min.

Bring milk to the boil and pour into saucepan, add salt and pepper to taste.

Simmer for 15-20 mins.

Blend in blender or pour through a fine sieve.

Mix beaten egg yolks and cream together to make liaison and add to saucepan.

Bring back just to the point of boiling, being careful not to boil.

Season to taste and garnish with the Asparagus Tips.

 Nutritional Advice: Asparagus is an excellent source of glutathione and beta-carotene (anti-oxidants) a good source of vitamin A & C and is rich in potassium and folic acid.

Suggested Wine: Rully or Spanish Rosè

Carrot and Coriander Soup

This soup is strengthening and energising and simple to make. Served with wholemeal bread it is a complete meal.

Serves 6

Ingredients

Gluten free

8 Carrots, thinly sliced
90g / 3 $\frac{1}{2}$oz / $\frac{1}{3}$Cup Butter
1 Onion, diced
1.7L / 3pt / 6 Cups Vegetable stock
2 lrg Potatoes, peeled and diced
1 Bunch of fresh coriander, chopped
Sea salt and pepper
125ml / 4floz / $\frac{1}{2}$Cup Créme fraîche

Method

CHEF'S TIP

If you scrub carrots well, there is no need to peel them.

Sauté carrots with butter, onion and potatoes until soft but not brown – about 15 mins.

Add stock, salt and pepper. Simmer until carrots are soft – about 30 mins.

Blend in blender or pour through a fine sieve.

Return to pan, add cream to coriander and 15g / 1tb / 1T of butter.

Check seasoning.

Garnish with coriander leaves and Crème fraîche.

 Nutritional Advice: Carrots are rich in Carotene-Beta and vitamin A.

Suggested Wine: Languedoc Merlot.

Creamy Asparagus Soup

Carrot and Coriander Soup

Kilkenny Seafood Chowder

Fish soups are usually made from lean fish. The flavour of the soup is more interesting if you use a great variety of fish. You can make an extremely good fish soup even if you have only frozen fish and fish stock to work with because the essential flavours are onions, leeks, garlic, herbs, carrots and potatoes.

Serves 6

Ingredients

1.2L / 2pt / 5Cups Fish stock
50g / 2oz / $^1/_4$Cup Butter
1 Onion finely chopped
1 Leek finely chopped
1 Carrot finely chopped
1 Stick of celery, chopped
3 med Potatoes, finely chopped
280ml / $^1/_2$pt / $1^1/_4$Cup Milk
175ml / 6floz / $^3/_4$Cup Cream
60gr / 2oz Plain flour or gluten-free flour
Bunch fresh dill or parsley, chopped
Salt and pepper
450g /1lb Salmon skinned, boned and cut into cubes
225g / 1/2lb Cod skinned, boned and cut into cubes
1 Packet seafood cocktail mix
Or
450g /1lb of a mixture of the following:
Fresh mussels, shrimp, calamaries, white haddock

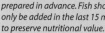

CHEF'S TIP

The stock for this soup can be prepared in advance. Fish should only be added in the last 15 mins to preserve nutritional value.

Gluten free

Method

Melt butter in saucepan. Add onion, leek, carrots, celery and potatoes. Cook over medium heat for 8 mins. until soft.
Stir in flour. Reduce heat to low and cook for 1 minute.
Add stock and season with salt and pepper. Bring just up to the boil and then reduce heat. Simmer for 15 mins., add fish and simmer for another 8 mins. until fish is cooked.
Stir in milk, cream and dill. Reheat, but do not boil.

 Nutritional Advice: Salmon is rich in Omega-3 fats. To reduce the risk of heart disease and stroke we should eat fish twice a week. Fish is excellent nourishment for the brain. Shellfish are rich in the mineral Zinc. Cod, haddock and whiting are good sources of low fat protein.

Suggested Wine: Alsace Pinot Blanc or White Burgundy such as Louis Max.

Kilkenny Seafood Chowder

Spanish Chorizo and Chickpea Soup

This rustic soup is practically a meal in itself and is perfect for cold winter days.

Serves 6-8

Ingredients
2 x 400g / 8oz Can cooked chickpeas drained
45ml / 3tb / 3T Olive oil
2 Leeks sliced thinly or diced
2 Onions diced
2 Carrots diced
2 Sticks celery diced
2 Potatoes diced
2 x 400g / 8oz Can chopped tomatoes
2 Cloves garlic chopped
1tsp / 1t Turmeric (ground)
1tsp / 1t Cumin (ground)
Salt and pepper
225gr / 8ozs Chorizo sausage diced
1.7L / 3pt / 7Cups Chicken stock

Method
Heat oil in a saucepan. Add spices, onions, garlic, leeks, carrots
and celery and cook gently for 15 mins. stirring occasionally.
Add chickpeas, potatoes, tomatoes, chorizo sausage and seasoning.
Cover and gently simmer for a further 15 mins.
It should be thick with vegetables, and contain very little liquid.
Serve piping hot with crusty bread.

 Nutritional Advice: Chickpeas contain valuable anti-oxidants which help to stimulate the immune system. They also help to lower cholesterol.

CHEF'S TIP
For a vegetarian option, leave out the chorizo and use vegetable stock.

Suggested Wine: Tempranillo

Spanish Chorizo and Chickpea Soup

Forest Mushroom Soup with Crème Fraîche

This is a very distinctive, creamy rich soup full of flavour.

Gluten free

Serves 6

Ingredients

1 lrg Onion finely diced
500g / 3tb / 3T Butter
500g / 3tb/ 3T Flour (gluten-free)
125g / 4floz / $^1/_2$Cup Fresh cream
1.1L / 2pt / 5Cups Boiling white stock (chicken or vegetable)
450g / 1lb / 5Cups Fresh mushrooms, sliced
125g / 4oz / 2Cups Mixed dried forest mushrooms – soaked and strained
Salt and pepper
5ml / 1tsp / 1t Lemon juice
5oz/ 4tb / 4T Chopped Parsley
50g / 3tb / 3T Crème fraîche
Chives for garnish

> **CHEF'S TIP**
> For richer soup, you could add 2 egg yolks to the cream and beat in soup by spoonful until a cupful has been added. Do not let the soup boil.

Method

Cook onion and mushroom stems slowly in butter until they are tender. Add the flour and cook for 1 min. without browning, add the parsley.
Off the heat. Blend in the boiling stock and blend it thoroughly with the flour. Season to taste. Add mushrooms and simmer slowly until mushrooms are tender. Add the cream, adjust seasoning.

To Garnish

Soften 8 sliced mushroom caps in butter and lemon juice.
Pour soup into soup bowls and decorate with mushrooms, chopped chives and Crème fraîche.

Pumpkin and Sweetcorn Chowder

Gluten free

Squash are a wonderful winter vegetable especially the pumpkin, with its association with Halloween, witches and all things magical. It is now widely available and makes delicious substantial meals, including soups, vegetables and tarts.

Ingredients

400g / 14oz / 2Cups Sweetcorn
110g / 4oz / $^2/_3$Cup Diced bacon
30ml / 2tb / 2T Olive oil
1 Onion diced
1 Carrot diced
1 Stick of celery diced
2 Cloves of garlic (minced)
1kg / 2lbs Pumpkin peeled, seeded,cubed
$^1/_4$tsp / $^1/_4$t Cinnamon
600ml / 1pt / 3Cups Chicken stock
150ml / $^1/_4$pt / $^2/_3$Cup Orange juice
6 Baby corn cooked and cut lengthways
15ml / 1tb / 1T Chopped coriander
Pinch of grated nutmeg, salt and pepper

Serves 6

Method

Heat a large saucepan, fry bacon until golden, remove and set aside. Add a little oil to saucepan and sauté all diced vegetables and garlic for about 8 mins. Stir in spices, add pumpkin, stock and orange juice.
Cover and bring to the boil. Reduce heat and simmer for 20 mins. until pumpkin is softened. Put half the soup in a food processor and blend until smooth. Add bacon and pour soup back into the saucepan. Add babycorn and coriander and heat gently, Season to taste.
Garnish with toasted pumpkin seeds and parmesan shavings.

Suggested Wine: Alsace Riesling, Chilean or South African Chardonnay.

Forest Mushroom Soup with Crème Fraîche

Vegetable Chowder with Gouda

Serves 6

Ingredients

30g / 2tb / 2T Butter

1 med Onion diced

225g / $^1/_2$lb / 2Cups potatoes, peeled and diced

225g / $^1/_2$lb / 2Cups chopped broccoli

225g / $^1/_2$lb / 2Cups diced carrots

225g / $^1/_2$lb / 4 Sticks diced celery

250ml / 8floz / 1Cup Milk

275ml/ $^1/_2$pt / 1$^1/_4$Cups Vegetable stock

50g / 2oz / 4T Plain or gluten-free flour

375g/ 13oz / 4Cups Grated gouda cheese

CHEF'S TIP

Do not overcook, vegetables should be firm when cooked.

Gluten free

Method

Melt butter in large saucepan. Cook and stir onion over medium heat until soft. Add carrots, potatoes and celery and cook until soft, about 5 mins.

Add broccoli, cauliflower and stock, bring to the boil and simmer for about 8 mins.

Whisk milk into flour until smooth, add to vegetables and cook stirring until mixture thickens.

Remove from heat and add grated cheese.

Serve with croutons and extra cheese.

Vegetable Chowder with Gouda

North African Aubergine and Couscous salad

In order to stay healthy we are advised to eat at least five portions of fruit or vegetables every day. There is nothing as easy to achieve in the kitchen as a good salad and they should be eaten all year round.

Serves 6

Ingredients

350g / 12oz / 2Cups Instant couscous
2 Aubergines
1 med Onion, halved and sliced
250ml / 8floz /1Cup Olive oil
3tsp / 3t Ground cumin
$^1/_4$tsp / $^1/_4$t Ground cinnamon
1tsp / 1t Paprika
$^1/_4$tsp / $^1/_4$t Ground cloves
30g / 1oz / 1Cup Fresh parsley, chopped
75g / 3oz / $^1/_3$Cup Butter
Salt and pepper

> **CHEF'S TIP**
>
> *This salad can be made in advance, just toss the ingredients together at the last minute. Be careful not to burn the onions or they will taste bitter.*

Method

Place couscous in large bowl and add 1pt/3Cups of boiling water. Leave for 5 to 10 mins then fluff up with a fork.

Cook onion in 2tb/2T of the oil until golden brown. Cut the aubergine into slices then into quarters and place in a large bowl, combine with the cumin, cinnamon, paprika, cloves and salt. Toss until well coated then cook in pan, over medium heat until browned. Remove from pan and cool.

Melt butter, add to couscous, stir in onions, aubergine and parsley.

 Nutritional Advice: Aubergines contain good amounts of potassium and folates, potatoes provide us with vitamin c and energy.

Mangetout in Walnut Dressing

Serves 6

Ingredients

450g / 16oz Mangetout (Snow Peas)
1 Red onion thinly cut
1 Red pepper cut very thinly
10 Babycorn cut in half and chargrilled
Zest and juice of one lemon
10 Walnuts
90ml / 2floz / $^1/_4$Cup Olive oil

> **CHEF'S TIP**
>
> *Your kitchen should have a salad spinner and an electric whisk, Balsamic vinegar from Modena, a good array of high quality oils and a selection of mustards, sea salt and black pepper.*

Method

Toast the walnuts on a dry pan until they start to change colour. Blend the nuts with the olive oil and lemon in a blender to make the dressing. Top and tail the mangetout and rinse under cold water, drain well. Toss the mangetout, red pepper, red onion and babycorn together and coat with the dressing.

The rest of the dressing will keep for a week or two in the fridge.

North African Aubergine and Coucous Salad

Bean and Lentil Salad with Salsa Dressing

This versatile and extremely basic recipe can be served chunky or blended to a velvet texture. Here we keep it chunky.
Serves 6

Ingredients
1 can / 400g / 8oz / 1Cup Cooked butter beans
1 can / 400g / 8oz / 2Cups Cooked cannellini beans
1 can / 400g / 8oz / 1Cup Cooked flageolet beans
1 can / 400g / 8oz / 1Cup Cooked kidney beans
1 can / 400g / 8oz / 1Cup Cooked chickpeas
1 can / 400g / 8oz / 2Cups Cooked puy or brown lentils

Salsa Dressing
Ingredients
2 Celery sticks, diced
Salt and cracked pepper
1 Green & yellow pepper diced
4 lrg Tomatoes, seeded and cut into cubes
1 Large red onion cut and diced
1 Clove of garlic, chopped finely
2 Chillies red or green seeded and diced.
2 Limes, zest and juice
1 Bunch of fresh coriander

Method
Drain and rinse beans and lentils, leave to drain while you prepare the dressing.
In a large bowl, combine all salsa ingredients and toss in beans and lentils. Cover and leave to marinate for 1 hour.
Season to taste.

 Nutritional Advice: Beans are an excellent source of protein and fibre, they also contain vitamin B and folic acid. Eaten in sufficient quantities, lentils control blood sugar levels and lower Cholesterol.
Lentils are virtually fat free and contain iron, potassium, magnesium and some of the B vitamins.

CHEF'S TIP

Always rinse tinned beans and lentils before use. They are a must in the kitchen cupboard as they are so versatile for last minute dishes.

Bean and Lentil Salad with Salsa Dressing

Crisp Carrot and Zucchini with Thyme Vinaigrette

Serves 6

This modest looking salad has its invisible charms.
An easy dish to prepare and it is very nutritious.

Ingredients

4 Carrots

4 Zucchini

Dressing

2tb / 2T Walnut oil

3tb / 3T Olive oil

1tb / 1T Chopped Thyme

Sea salt and freshly ground pepper

CHEF'S TIP
To reduce calories, fresh lemon juice and zest may be used instead of oil for the dressing.

Method

Whisk all dressing ingredients together until smooth and set aside.

Wash, peel and grate carrots coarsely.

Wash and grate zucchini coarsely.

In a large bowl, combine dressing with carrots and zucchini and sprinkle with thyme leaves.

 Nutritional Advice: Raw Carrots are a excellent source of vitamin A. Raw zucchini are a good source of vitamin C. Both contain the anti-oxident beta carotene.

Crisp Carrot and Zucchini with Thyme Vinaigrette

Spiced Carrot and Pistachio Nuts with Orange Dressing

Spiced Carrot and Pistachio Nuts with Orange Dressing

Ingredients

Serves 6

4 Large Carrots

50g / 2oz / $^1/_3$Cup Raisins

30g / 2tb / 2T Chopped pistachio nuts

3 Cardamon pods

5ml / 1tsp / 1t Black mustard seeds

5ml / 1tsp / 1t Ground ginger

5ml / 1tsp / 1t Ground cumin

5ml / 1tsp / 1t Ground coriander

5ml / 1tsp / 1t Paprika

80ml / 3floz / $^1/_4$Cup Olive oil

2tb / 2T Orange juice, keep zest
for garnish

275g / 10oz / $1^1/_4$Cups of thick
plain yoghurt

1tsp / 1t Orange juice

Method

Roast pistachio nuts for 8 mins. in oven at
180^C/350^f/gas 4

Peel and coarsely grate the carrots.

Crush the cardamon pod to extract the seeds.

Heat a frying pan on low heat and cook the mustard
seeds until they pop. Add in the cumin, ginger, paprika,
cardamon seeds, coriander and heat for a few seconds,
remove and stir in the oil, juices and raisins until well
combined.

Pour dressing over carrots and leave for 20 mins. Pile
salad into serving dish and garnish with the chopped
pistachios. Mix the orange juice and yoghurt in a bowl
and garnish with orange zest.

Serve yoghurt separately.

CHEF'S TIP

*Use any dried fruit of your
choice, finely shredded or
diced instead of raisins.*

Nutritional Advice: Eating nuts helps to reduce the risk of heart disease. Because of their high
fat content they are best eaten as the protein part of the meal.

Mixed Tomato and Broad Bean Salad with Lemon Dressing

Serves 6

Ingredients

225g / 8oz Yellow cherry tomatoes
225g / 8oz Red cherry tomatoes
350g / 12oz Broad beans (frozen)
50ml / 2floz / $3^1/_2$T Olive oil
Bunch fresh parsley
Sea salt & cracked pepper
1 Clove garlic
Zest and juice of 1 lemon

CHEF'S TIP
Place cooked vegetables for salads in iced water, this helps to restore the vibrant colours.

Method

Cook beans until tender in salted boiling water for 8-10 mins. Rinse under ice cold water and drain well.

Cut tomatoes in half, chop parsley and add all the ingredients together in a bowl and mix.

Toss in the lemon dressing and taste for seasoning.

Lemon Dressing

Combine garlic, lemon juice & zest, olive oil, salt and pepper until well blended

 Nutritional Advice: Tomatoes are a good source of lycopene, an anti-oxidant which can protect against heart disease.

Watermelon, Feta and Watercress Salad

Serves 6

Ingredients

1 sml Watermelon
200g / 7oz / 1Cup Feta cheese cut into cubes
2 Bunches of watercress leaves

Dressing

90ml / 6tb / 6T Extra virgin olive oil
45ml / 3tb / 3T Fresh lemon Juice
$1/_2$ tsp / $1/_2$t Dried oregano

CHEF'S TIP
Don't add any salt as feta cheese is quite salty.

Method

Whisk the dressing ingredients together in a small bowl.

Remove the flesh of the watermelon and cut into cubes.

Place the watermelon, feta and watercress leaves in a large serving bowl.

Toss with dressing and serve immediately as the watercress will begin to wilt as soon as the dressing is added.

 Nutritional Advice: Watercress contains large amounts of sulphur and is a good body cleanser.

Mixed Tomato and Broad Bean Salad with Lemon Dressing

Prawn Noodle Salad

A highly nutritious and delicious Asian dish.
Serves 6

Ingredients
6 Babycorn sliced in half
75g / 3oz / $^1/_2$Cup peanuts or cashew nuts
315g / 10oz Egg noodles
5 Spring onions (cut into thin lengths)
25g / 8oz Mangetout (Snow Peas)
1 medium Red Pepper (thinly sliced)
1 medium Yellow pepper (thinly sliced)
225g / 8oz / 1$^1/_2$Cups Cooked peeled prawns
Chopped coriander
Salt and pepper
Dressing
Ingredients
1 Clove of garlic crushed
1 Green chilli minced
1 Red chilli minced
10ml / 2 tsp / 2t White sugar
150ml / 5floz / $^2/_3$Cup Soya sauce
30ml / 2tb / 2T Sesame seed oil
30ml / 2tb / 2T Olive oil
15ml / 1tb / 1T White wine vinegar
1 tsp / 1t Brown sugar
2 tsp / 2t Grated fresh ginger

> **CHEF'S TIP**
>
> Grow your own herbs and salad leaves in a window box and you will always have fresh herbs available in your Kitchen.

Method
Put all the ingredients for the dressing into a bowl and blend well together.
Cook noodles in boiling salted water for about 5 mins. Add a drop of oil to water and stir well to help separate the noodles. Drain and rinse under cold water and drain again.
Lightly fry the peppers and add the spring onion and fry for 1 min. Remove from the heat and set aside.
Add the babycorn and cook on high heat until golden.
When the noodles are cold add the mangetout, prawns, coriander, nuts and babycorn. Add dressing and toss well.
Sprinkle with some chopped coriander and chillies.

 Nutritional Advice: Eating chillies helps maintain good brain function, ginger is also known to stimulate the brain. This salad contains both.

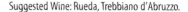

Suggested Wine: Rueda, Trebbiano d'Abruzzo.

Prawn Noodle Salad

Roast Zucchini, Chickpea and Couscous Salad

Serves 6

Ingredients
350g / 12oz / 2Cups Instant couscous
425g / 8oz / 1 Can chickpeas, drained and rinsed
1 Red pepper
75g / 30oz / $^3/_4$Cup Chopped pistachios
3 Zucchini
2 Spring onions finely sliced
50g / 3tb / 3T Fresh mint, shredded
Salt and pepper

Dressing
Ingredients
15ml / 3tsp Cumin seeds (toasted)
2 Cloves garlic (finely chopped)
1 sml Red chilli, seeds removed and chopped
125g / 4floz / $^1/_2$Cup Lemon juice
125g / 4floz / $^1/_2$Cup Extra virgin olive oil

> **CHEF'S TIP**
>
> *Couscous is a Middle Eastern staple dish, made from Semolina. This salad is a delicious accompaniment to grilled lamb and chicken.*

Method
Cook red pepper under hot grill or in oven at 200^C/400^f/gas 6 until skin blackens and blisters. Cover until cool, remove skin and membrane and cut into thin strips.
Roast pistachio nuts for 5 to 8 mins. until lightly golden. Chop roughly.
Thinly slice the zucchini, drizzle with oil, pan fry or grill until golden.
Place couscous in large bowl, cover with 3 cups of boiling water and leave for 10 mins. Toss with fork to remove any lumps.
Add nuts, chickpeas, red pepper, spring onion, mint and toss well.
Pour dressing over salad to combine.
Season to taste
Dressing
Method
Place the cumin seeds in a dry pan and toast gently for 1-2 mins.
Mix with the garlic, chilli, lemon juice and oil.
Add sea salt and cracked pepper.
Gently toss the dressing with all the salad ingredients.

Roast Zucchini, Chickpea and Couscous Salad

Nicoise Salad

Gluten free

Serves 6

Ingredients
900g / 2 lbs sml New potatoes (skins on)
450g / 1lb / 2Cups Tuna chunks
450g / 1lb Thin green beans
250g / 8oz / $1^2/_3$Cup Kalamata olives
Sea salt
Freshly cracked black pepper

Garnish: Sprig of fresh thyme

CHEF'S TIP
This salad will store very well if you have to make it in advance. Just refrigerate until ready to serve.

Dressing
Ingredients
50g / 2oz / $^1/_2$Cup Chopped flat parsley
3tb / 3T Lemon juice
2tb / 2T White wine vinegar
3tb / 3T Dry white wine (optional)
1tsp / 1t Fine sea salt
120ml / 4 floz / $^1/_2$Cup Extra virgin olive oil
1tsp / 1t Freshly ground black pepper
1tsp / 1t Chopped fresh thyme leaves
1 med Red onion, finely diced

Dressing
Mix lemon juice, white wine, white wine vinegar, thyme leaves, mustard, salt and pepper. Whisk in the oil, red onion and parsley.

Method
Boil, steam or microwave potatoes until tender. Drain, cool and cut into quarters.
Cook beans in boiling water for a maximum of 2 mins. until just crisp and tender.
Run under cold water to preserve the colour, drain well.
In a large bowl, combine green beans, olives, potatoes and tuna chunks.
Pour the dressing over and mix gently until ingredients are thoroughly coated.
Add salt and pepper to taste, transfer to serving dish and garnish with a sprig of thyme.

Suggested Wine: Cote de Provence or Bandol Rosè

Nicoise Salad

Baby New Potato Spanish Salad

Gluten free

From the land of the Gazpacho, a tomato based dressing turns this simple salad into a particularly refreshing side dish
Serves 6

Ingredients
700g / 2$^1/_4$lbs / 7Cups Baby new potatoes

Dressing
3 lrg Tomatoes, de-seeded and dried
1 lrg Red pepper
1 Clove of garlic, peeled and chopped
1 med Red onion, cut into small dice
60ml / 4tb / 4T Olive oil
15ml / 3tsp / 3t Red wine vinegar
50g / 2oz / 1Cup Flat leaf parsley
Sea salt and cracked pepper

CHEF'S TIP
Preserved jars of roasted red peppers can be easily found in most supermarkets.

Method
Scrub and wash potatoes, leave skins on.
Bring a pot of water to boiling point. Add potatoes and salt. Return to the boil and boil until tender for about 10-12 mins.

Meanwhile prepare dressing.
Cook red pepper in oven at 200^C/400^f/gas 6 or grill until skin blackens and blisters. Cover and cool. Remove skin and membrane. Dice pepper and set aside.

In a large bowl, combine all dressing ingredients and toss in the potatoes and red pepper, sprinkle with flat leaf parsley.

Serve warm or cold.

Suggested Wine: Italian dry Muscadet.

Baby New Potato Spanish Salad

Okra, Green Bean and Crispy Bacon Salad

Serves 6

 Gluten free

Ingredients

200g / 7oz Okra
200g / 7oz French bean
200g / 7oz Mangetout (Snow Peas)
6 Slices of crispy bacon
Finely chopped basil and rocket

Dressing (French)

15ml / 1tb / 1T Red wine vinegar
$^1/_8$tsp / $^1/_8$t Fine sea salt
$^1/_2$tsp / $^1/_2$t Ground black pepper
60ml / 4tb / 4T Extra virgin olive oil
5ml / 1tsp / 1t Dijon mustard

Method

Blanch okra in boiling water for 3 mins.
Blanch mangetout and french beans in boiling water for 2 mins.
Rinse in a lot of cold water and drain well.
Cook bacon until really crispy then finely chop.
Mix all ingredients with dressing.

CHEF'S TIP

For a vegetarian option leave out the bacon and add pinenuts instead.

 Nutritional Advice: Okra is excellent for digestion.

Italian Rice Salad

Serves 6

Gluten free

Ingredients

300g / 11oz / 1$^1/_2$Cups Wild rice mix
175g / 6oz / 1Cup Sweetcorn
225g / 8oz / 1Cup Mixed beans (cooked)
50g / 2oz / $^1/_2$Cup Rocket

Dressing

6 Gherkins
6 Black olives
4 Sunblushed tomatoes
100ml / 4floz / $^2/_3$Cup Olive oil
2tb / 2T White wine vinegar
Salt and pepper

Method

Cook rice for about 20-30 mins. Rinse well in cold water and drain.
Rinse sweetcorn and beans.
Place all ingredients in a bowl with roughly chopped rocket. Keep some back for garnish.
Mix all dressing ingredients in a food processor and pour over. Sprinkle with rocket.

German Potato Salad

Serves 6

Ingredients

6 Cooked (boiled) and diced potato
1 Chopped red onion
8-10 Capers
6-8 Cooked diced smoked sausages
150ml / 5floz / $^2/_3$Cup French dressing (see recipe above)

Method

Mix well in a large bowl, add the dressing and season to taste.

CHEF'S TIP

This potato salad can be prepared in advance and kept refrigerated for up to two days.
Omit sausages for vegetarian option.

 Nutritional Advice: Wild rice is brown-black in colour, chewier than long grain white rice it has a distinctive nutty flavour. It is gluten-free and contains twice as much protein, iron and calcium as brown rice.

Okra, Green Bean and Crispy Bacon Salad / German Potato Salad

Italian Rice Salad

Coriander, Babycorn and Soya Oriental Salad

Serves 6

Ingredients
500g / 2oz / $^1/_2$Cup Walnuts
6 Babycorn
2 Red peppers
1 Red onion
450g / 16 oz Mangetout
Juice of 1 Lemon
Salt and pepper
1lrg Bunch of coriander (chopped)
50ml / 2floz / 4T Olive oil
25ml / 1floz / 1$^1/_2$T Soy sauce

> **CHEF'S TIP**
>
> *You can substitute sugar snap peas for the mangetout. For best results make just before serving.*

Method
Thinly slice the red peppers and onion and set aside.
Rinse the mangetout and top and tail.
Cut the babycorn in half lenghtways, fry in dry pan and set aside.
Roast the walnuts in the oven for 6 mins at 180^C/ 350^f/gas 5.
When cool, blend nuts, olive oil, lemon juice and soy sauce together in a blender until smooth and season to taste.
Add the coriander and toss all the ingredients together.
Garnish with coriander leaves and serve.

Suggested Wine: Spanish Sauvignon Blanc

Spinach, Bacon and Pine Nuts Salad with Roasted Red Pepper Dressing

> **CHEF'S TIP**
>
> *As an alternative to spinach you will find that rocket or mixed leaves will work well in this recipe.*

Serves 6
Ingredients
250g / 8oz / 2Cups Baby spinach-washed and dried
6 Rashers / Bacon
90gr / 3oz $^1/_3$Cup Pine nuts toasted
Dressing
2 Red peppers
3tb / 3T Olive oil
1tb / 1T Balsamic vinegar
1 Lime, zest and juice
Salt and pepper

Method
To prepare dressing:
Roast Peppers until charred, cover and when cool peel off skin and remove seeds, preserve any juices.
Toss all ingredients in blender until smooth.
Cook rashers until crispy and cut into small pieces.
Roast Pine Nuts until just turning brown or just until you can faintly smell them.
Combine rashers, pine nuts (when cool) with the dressing, toss in the spinach and serve immediately.

 Nutritional Advice: Spinach is an excellent source of folate, calcium and iron.

Coriander, Babycorn and Soya Oriental Salad

Tabbouleh

A highly nutritious and delicious Middle-Eastern dish.

Serves 6

Ingredients

175g / 6oz / 1Cup Bulgar wheat

6 Spring onions finely chopped

200g / 7oz / 1^1/$_2$Cup Parsley

125g / 4oz / 1Cup Fresh mint

50ml / 2floz / ^{1}/$_4$Cup Lemon juice and zest

50ml / 2floz / ^{1}/$_4$Cup Olive oil

3 Tomatoes

Salt and pepper

Method

CHEF'S TIP

Serve tabbouleh in a toasted pitta pocket for a great snack.

Finely prepare Bulgar wheat in a large bowl and pour in enough boiling water to cover. Leave to soak for about 20mins.

Meanwhile prepare your spring onions by chopping finely. Chop the parsley and mint finely.

Prepare lemon juice and zest.

Chop the tomatoes in small dice, reserving the juices.

Combine all of the above with the Bulgar wheat, mix in the olive oil, tomato juice and plenty of salt and cracked pepper.

 Nutritional Advice: A great salad for vegetarians, high in fibre and rich in iron, protein and minerals.

Tabbouleh

Vegetable Dishes

Goats Cheese Tartlet with
Sun-blushed Tomatoes and Zucchini

A delicious tartlet, quick and easy to prepare. We serve this in the restaurant with mixed leaves, Swiss chard, rocket and lollo rosso.

Ingredients

375g / 13oz / $3^1/_3$Cups Goat's cheese
18 Sun-blushed tomatoes
3 Leeks sliced thinly
1 lrg Zucchini sliced
1 Jar Ready-made hollandaise sauce
1 Egg (for glazing)
375g / 13oz Puff pastry (ready rolled)

Method

Firstly prepare the pastry case with the puff pastry.
Preheat oven to 200^C/400^f/gas 6.
Lay the pastry out flat on a work surface. Cut into 6 squares or rectangles, score the borders and knock up the edges. Prepare glaze by beating the egg with a teaspoon of water.
Place the pastry on a tray and let it rest in fridge for 10 mins. This reduces shrinkage when baking. Place pastry on a wet baking sheet, glaze with egg wash and bake for 10 mins. until golden and puffy.

Sauté the leeks in a little butter until just tender. Set aside.
Grill or sauté zucchini on both sides.

To assemble tarts:
When pastry shells are ready tap down the centre very gently and place the leek first. Arrange 3 sunblushed tomatoes on the sides, add the zucchini and then the goats cheese. Top it off with tablespoon of hollandaise sauce.
Place in a pre-heated oven 200^C/400^f/gas 6 for 8 mins. until the sauce starts to bubble.
Sprinkle with basil and serve.

 Nutritional Advice: Salad leaves offer very high anti-oxidant content, as does zucchini which is a source of vitamin c and is also low in calories.

Suggested Wine: Menetou Salon Blanc

Goats Cheese Tartlet with Sun-blushed Tomatoes and Zucchini

Cherry Tomato, Artichoke and Gruyérè Cheese Frittata

An interesting and flavoursome dish which is ideal for lunch or light suppers. Great warm or cold with salads.

Serves 6

Ingredients
You will need a 20cm / 8in non-stick ovenproof pan
18 Cherry tomatoes
225g / 8oz / 2Cups Artichoke hearts in oil (drained)
10 med Eggs
3tb / 3T Double cream or crème fraîche
30g / 1oz / 2T Freshly grated parmesan
150g / 5 oz / 1Cup Gruyérè cheese, cut into cubes
1 sml Onion, finely diced
10 Basil leaves
Sea salt and cracked pepper

> **CHEF'S TIP**
>
> *Gruyere cheese must be used in this recipe because of its robust taste.*

Method
Pre-heat oven to 180^C/350^f/gas 4.
Sauté the onions in oil until soft. Drain the artichokes and cut into quarters. Whisk egg with the cream, seasoning and parmesan cheese. Slice the cherry tomatoes in half or leave whole.
Place tomatoes and artichokes on top of the onions. Top with the Gruyere and basil. Pour over egg mixture. Cook over a medium heat for 6 mins. then transfer to the oven, preheated to 180^C/350^f/gas 4.
Cook for approximately 30 mins. until golden and set. Serve warm or cold.

Suggested Wine: Light fruity wine, German or Austrian.

Broccoli Purée with Parmesan and Nutmeg

Serves 6

Ingredients
1kg / 3lbs Broccoli or 2 lrg Bunches
100g / 4oz / $^1/_2$Cup Butter diced
80g / 3oz / $^2/_3$Cup Parmesan cheese
$^1/_4$tsp / $^1/_4$t Nutmeg

> **CHEF'S TIP**
>
> *This makes a good side dish for poultry.*

Method
Cut off stems from broccoli and set aside. Steam or boil broccoli stems for about 6 mins. Add broccoli florets. Cook until just tender for about 5min., reserving some florets for garnish. Drain well. Add butter and purée until smooth.
Blend in the cheese and nutmeg. Season with salt and pepper.

Cherry Tomato, Artichoke and Gruyérè Cheese Frittata

Tomato and Red Onion Bruschetta

Serves 4

Ingredients

2 Demi-baguettes or 4 Crusty dinner rolls (long)
8 lrg Tomatoes cut in quarters with seeds taken out
30ml / 2 tb / 2T of Kilkenny basil pesto oil
1 med Red onion
6 Fresh basil leaves
Salt and pepper

CHEF'S TIP
Serving the mix on small slices of toast make an interesting canapé for parties or pre-dinner drinks.

Method

Take the bread and cut it lengthways. If you are using baguettes, cut them in half first. Finely chop the tomato and onion into small dice, add the pesto oil, mix and season.

Place the breads under a hot grill to toast very lightly. Then divide the tomato mix equally between the toasted breads and return to the grill for just about 30 seconds. Serve immediately with some fresh chopped basil leaves to garnish.

Tomato and Red Onion Bruschetta

Stuffed Field Mushrooms with Basil Oil

Stuffed Field Mushrooms with Basil Oil

Serves 4

Ingredients

8 med or 1 lrg Open flat
 mushroom
1 med Red onion
2 Cloves of garlic
1Tb / 1T Fresh parsley
6 Slices of stale white bread
100g / 3$^{1}/_{2}$ oz Mixed salad leaves
50g / 2oz / $^{1}/_{4}$Cup Melted butter

Dressing (basil oil)

100ml / 4floz / 7 T Olive oil (extra
virgin, if available)
25g / 1oz / 1T Fresh basil, finely
chopped
Salt and pepper

Method

Wipe clean, peel and remove the stalks from the mushrooms, cut the onions into quarters. Set aside. Peel garlic cloves and wash the parsley. Cut the crusts off the bread and cut into quarters. Now put garlic, parsley, bread and onion into a food processor and blitz until the mixture is blended into a crumb like texture. Then add the melted butter to bind. Stuff the mushrooms with this mixture. Now place them in a preheated oven on a greased tray at 180^C/350^f/gas 4 for approximately 8 mins., or until the stuffing is golden brown. While the mushrooms are in the oven, mix together the basil oil ingredients with a hand blender until the herbs are well blended through the oil (30-60 secs.). This will keep in the fridge for up to 3 days so can be made in advance or used for other dishes, or as a delicious salad dressing. When the mushrooms are cooked, serve immediately with a gener-ous drizzle of the oil and salad leaves, if desired.

Escalavida

This is a great salad for summer or winter and is very popular with our regular customers. It also travels well for picnics.

Serves 6

Method

Ingredients
6 Baby or 2 lrg Aubergines
6 Tomatoes
2 Red peppers
2 Yellow peppers
2 Zucchini
4 med Potatoes

Dressing
100g / 4oz Sun-dried tomatoes
30ml / 1floz / 2T Olive oil
30g / 1oz / 2T Parsley
2 Cloves of garlic

Blend the dressing ingredients together in a blender to a course consistency. Pre-heat oven 180^C/350^f/gas 4.

Cut Aubergines, zucchini and peppers into large chunky pieces.

Skin tomatoes by dropping into boiling water for 60 secs. Remove, peel off skin and cut in half.

Peel potatoes and cut in quarters.

Blend together salad ingredients and dressing. Add salt and cracked pepper.

Place in roasting pan and cook at 180^C/350^f/gas 4 for 40 mins.

Can be served cold or warm.

Escalavida

Fusilli Pasta

Fusilli Pasta

Serves 6

Ingredients

315g / 10oz / $2^1/_2$Cups Fusilli
90g / 3oz Parmesan Cheese (Shavings)
125g / 4oz Sunblushed tomatoes
Sea salt and cracked Pepper
1lrg Bunch basil leaves (save some for garnish)
140ml / 5floz / $^2/_3$Cup Olive oil
2 Cloves of garlic
3tb / 3T Balsamic vinegar

Method
Bring a pot of water to boiling point, add a $^1/_2$ tps of salt.
Add Fusilli, boil rapidly until al dente, about 10 mins.
Drain and refresh under cold water. Drain well.
Cut salami into thin strips.
Prepare parmesan shavings using a vegetable peeler.
Prepare dressing in blender.
Toss in sunblushed tomatoes, garlic, basil, salt, pepper, balsamic vinegar and olive oil.
Do not over blend, keep it chunky.
Combine all ingredients together with dressing.
Scatter over Parmesan shavings and basil leaves.

 Nutritional Advice: Pasta is a particularly healthy fast food whether dried or fresh. It contains fibre, proteinand vitamin B.

Suggested Wine: Lugana

Potato Nicoise

Serves 6

Ingredients

4 Fennel bulbs
450g / 1^1/$_4$ lbs. New potatoes
5tb / 5T Olive oil
Salt and pepper

Dressing Ingredients

10 Basil leaves
10 Black olives
Juice of 1 Lemon
6tb / 6T Olive oil
1 Clove garlic
3 Red peppers
Salt and pepper

Method

Cook potatoes in salted boiling water until just tender. Drain and leave to one side.
Cook fennel in salted boiling water for 5mins. and drain well.
While potatoes and fennel are cooking, prepare the dressing.
Roast and skin red peppers and dice finely. Peel and chop garlic or crush in a mortar with the salt. Dice black olives.
Stir in remaining ingredients and set aside.
Heat a ridged grill pan. Coat fennel and potatoes in olive oil. Cook on pan until well browned.
Toss salad dressing over and serve hot.

Roast Tikka Potatoes

Serves 6

Ingredients

800g / 2lb sml Potatoes peeled
30ml / 2floz / ^{1}/$_4$Cup Oil
1tsp / 1t Black mustard seeds
1tsp / 1t Coriander seeds
1Tsp / 1t Black onion seeds
5cm / 2in Piece of ginger chopped finely
6 Fresh or 4 Dried curry leaves
2 Red chillies de-seeded and sliced
1Tsp / 1t Turmeric
Salt and pepper

Method

Cook potatoes in salted boiling water until tender and drain well. Meanwhile prepare spices. In a large pan cook spices, ginger, curry leaves and chillies. Add potatoes. Place in an oven proof dish until potatoes are golden, about 15-20 mins.

Aloo Chat

Serves 6

Ingredients

30ml / 2floz / ^{1}/$_4$Cup Oil
1 sml Onion, finely chopped
450g / 1lb sml Waxy potatoes skinned and cut in half lengthways.
2 sml Red chillies, de-seeded and thinly sliced
2tsp / 2t Ground turmeric
3tsp / 3t Ground coriander
2tsp / 2t Cumin seeds, toasted in frying pan
500ml / 16floz / 2Cups Water
Fresh coriander leaves to garnish.

Method

Heat oil in a saucepan, add onions and cook for five mins. Add potatoes, chilli, turmeric, coriander, cumin seeds and cook until potatoes are nicely browned.
Add the water and bring to the boil. Reduce heat to simmer and cook until all liquid has been absorbed and potatoes are tender.
Serve hot, warm or cold as a salad.

> **CHEF'S TIP**
>
> *These potato dishes are of Indian origin. They are delicious and easy to prepare and all the ingredients are available in good supermarkets.*

Suggested Wine: For all three recipes. Rosè, Spanish or Chilean.

Potato Nicoise

Aloo Chat

Roast Tikka Potatoes

Tomato and Zucchini Bake

Serves 6

Ingredients

1 med Aubergine, peeled and chopped
2 med Onions, chopped
2 Cloves of garlic, crushed
125ml / 4floz / $\frac{1}{2}$Cup Extra virgin olive oil
2 med Zucchini, sliced diagonally
6 med Ripe tomatoes, sliced
Sprigs of herbs, oregon, rosemary
100g / 4oz / 1Cup Grated parmesan cheese
Cracked black pepper and salt

CHEF'S TIP

Use any fresh herbs you have to enhance this simple dish.

Method

Preheat oven to 200^C/400^f/gas 6.
Sprinkle the salt on the aubergine and leave in a colander for 30 mins. Drain and pat dry. Cook onion and garlic over medium heat until browned slightly. Transfer to baking dish and set aside.
Cook aubergine until tender and slightly browned. Add to onion mixture and place in a baking dish.
Arrange zucchini and tomatoes with the parmesan cheese, in layers over the aubergine mixture. Sprinkle herbs, drizzle over oil, season with pepper and bake until lightly golden on top.
To serve, sprinkle with cheese.

Tomato and Zucchini Bake

Meat Dishes

Greek Style Lamb with Tomato Rice

Serves 4

Ingredients

900g / 2lbs Diced lean leg or shoulder of lamb
1 Bottle Red wine
1Tb / 1T Fresh coriander
2 Bay leaves
50g / 2oz / $^{1}/_{4}$Cup Pitted black olives
225g / 8oz / 1$^{1}/_{2}$Cups Red Cherry tomatoes
2 med Onions, peeled and chopped
250ml / 9floz / 1$^{1}/_{4}$ Cups Tomato juice
Parsley and lime to garnish

Rice

250g / 9oz / 1$^{1}/_{2}$Cups Long grain easy cook rice
250ml / 9floz / 1$^{1}/_{4}$Cups Tomato juice
250ml/ 9floz / 1$^{1}/_{4}$Cups Water
Pinch of salt

> **CHEF'S TIP**
>
> *If you don't like the olives, replace them with chunks of red pepper and celery.*

Method

Marinate the lamb overnight with the onions, the chopped coriander, the bay leaves, the olives, the tomato juice and red wine. To cook, put the meat and marinade in a covered casserole dish and cook at 180^{c}/350^{f}/gas 4 for 2 hours. Uncover the casserole add the cherry tomatoes and continue cooking for 30 mins. more.

For the rice, heat the water and the tomato juice and when boiling add the rice and simmer for 10 mins. or until soft and the liquid is absorbed. Add salt to taste. Serve the lamb on a bed of the rice with a wedge of lime and some chopped parsley.

Suggested Wine: A good Greek or Bordeaux Red or a Bordeaux Rosè in summer.

Greek Style Lamb with Tomato Rice

Red Cooked Pork with Char-siu Sauce and Noodles

Serves 6

Ingredients

1¹/₂kg / 3lbs Shoulder or butt pork

500g / 1lb Noodles

1 Red pepper

1Green pepper

1 Yellow pepper

1 Garlic clove crushed

1 tsp / 1t Grated fresh ginger

1Tb / 1T Peanut oil

2Tb / 2T Honey

1Tb / 1T Light soy sauce

Garnish

30g / 10oz or Cellophane or glass noodles

Marinade

60ml / 2floz / ¹/₄Cup Hoisin sauce

60ml / 2floz / ¹/₄Cup Yellow bean curd sauce

30ml / 1floz Red bean curd cheese

30ml / 1floz / 2T Shoaxing wine (Chinese wine) or sherry

1tsp / 1t Salt

6Tb / 6T Sugar

3 Garlic cloves crushed

60ml / 2floz / ¹/₄Cup Soy sauce

> ### CHEF'S TIP
>
> *For Garnish, deep fry cellophane noodles for 60 seconds in hot oil and drain.*
> *Left over pork is great chopped into fried rice, but should be used within two days.*

Method

Blend all marinade ingredients together. Set aside.

Prepare pork by piercing several times and score every 5cm/2in with sharp knife.

Combine Pork in large bowl with marinade.

Mix well and refrigerate overnight.

Drain the pork well and reserve marinade.

Place the pork on a wire rack over a baking dish, to which you will add warm water in order to catch all the fat from the pork.

Roast uncovered in hot oven at 200^C/400^f/gas 6 for 30 mins.

Baste and reduce heat to 180^C/ 375^f/gas 4 for 1 hour or until pork is tender and cooked through, basting occasionally with marinade and add more water to dish.

Soften honey and pour over pork, cook for a further 10 mins.

Stand Pork for 10 mins. before slicing, keep warm while you prepare the sauce.

Empty the liquid contents from the baking dish into a clean saucepan, re-heat and season to taste.

While pork is cooking, Prepare the noodles according to instructions on packet. Add a little light soy sauce.

Thinly slice peppers, crush garlic and grate ginger.

Toss all in hot oil for 2 mins. and add to noodles.

To serve, arrange noodles on serving plate, place sliced pork on top.

Suggested Wine: Beaujolais Crus or new world Pinot Noir

Red Cooked Pork with Char-siu Sauce and Noodles

Kilkenny Irish Stew

Traditional Irish stew is made from shoulder of lamb or middle neck with just potatoes, parsley and onions. Here we include both celery and carrots.

Serves 6

Ingredients

1$^1/_2$kg / 3lb Shoulder of lamb or middle neck
450g / 1lb Onions
3 Potatoes cut in half or quartered
1 Head of celery
6 Carrots
1 lrg Bunch of parsley and rosemary or thyme
Salt and pepper

CHEF'S TIP
Cook extra potatoes separately.

Method

You will need a large saucepan.

Cut the lamb into cubes. Peel and cut onions into quarters. Place potatoes and onions in saucepan, cover with a layer of meat. Season with salt and pepper, parsley and rosemary or thyme. Continue to layer and season until all meat has been added (at this stage you can continue to cook the stew on top of the cooker or transfer to a casserole dish and cook it in the oven at 160^c/325^f/gas 3). Add enough water or stock to cover and bring to the boil. Skim away froth and lower heat to simmer. Cover and cook for 1 hour.

Meanwhile, prepare carrots and celery. Cut into barrel shapes about 3cm/1$^1/_4$in and add to stew. Continue cooking for 1 hour more.

 Nutritional Advice: You could also add a little barley for thickening and extra nutrition.

Kilkenny Irish Stew

69

Lamb Shank

Lamb Shank

Serves 6

Ingredients

6 Lamb shanks
175ml / 6floz / $^3/_4$Cup Olive oil
3 Cloves of garlic crushed
450g / 8oz / $1^1/_2$Cups Chopped tomatoes
1 lrg Onion chopped finely
1 Carrot chopped finely
6 Sprigs of parsley
3 Sprigs of rosemary
2 Bay leaves
8 Peppercorns
500ml / 1pt / 2Cups Chicken stock
22tb / 2T Honey

Method

Heat oil in a large ovenproof dish. Brown the shanks and set aside.

In the same dish add the garlic, onions and carrot and cook for about 8 mins.

Add the stock, tomatoes, peppercorns, bay leaf, parsley and rosemary. Season with salt and pepper. Return lamb shanks to the dish and bring to the boil. Drizzle the honey over, cover tightly and place in the oven for 2 hours at 180^C/350^f/gas 4 until the meat is tender.

Take out the shanks. Cover to keep warm while you prepare the sauce. Strain the juices and season. Reheat the sauce before serving.

Serve with creamed potatoes.

CHEF'S TIP

We complement the lamb shank with sweet potato purée, pearl onions and petit pois.

Suggested Wine: Bordeaux Rouge.

70

Braised Beef Casserole with Irish Stout

This is a rich casserole, an excellent family meal and can be prepared in advance which will allow the flavours to mature.

Serves 6

Ingredients
$1^1/_2$kg / 3lbs Good quality round steak
450g / 1lb 5Cups Button mushrooms
3Tb / 3T Plain flour
500ml / 1pt /2Cups Irish stout
500ml / 1pt / 2Cups Beef stock
1 Clove garlic
A lrg Bouquet garni
250g / 8oz Button mushrooms
125ml / 4floz / $^1/_2$Cup Oil

> **CHEF'S TIP**
>
> *The meat should be well browned before the liquid is added. Using a heavy pan is essential and should be large enough to hold the meat without overcrowding. The sauce should not be too thick but have good body and a well rounded flavour.*

Method
Prepare the meat by cutting into cubes. Peel and crush the garlic. Prepare stock.
Brown meat in batches, remove and set aside. De-glaze the pan with the flour. Add the stout and cook stirring constantly to reduce slightly then add the garlic and return meat to pan. Add stock.
Pop in you bouquet garni and cover, simmer gently for 15 mins.
Prepare onions, peel and glaze slightly on pan. Clean mushrooms (leave whole) and add to beef. Add the onions.
At this stage you can transfer the meat to a casserole dish and continue cooking in the oven for 2 hours at 180^C/350^f/gas 4.

Suggested Wine: Medium priced Bordeaux Rouge from the Haut-Medoc

Braised Beef Casserole with Irish Stout

Beef Lasagne with Buffalo Mozzarella

Serves 6
Ingredients
250g / 8 oz Fresh lasagne sheets
60ml / 2oz / $^1/_2$Cup Parmesan cheese, grated
2 Balls fresh buffalo mozzarella cheese sliced
Bunch of basil chopped
30 g/ 2Tb / 2T Butter
Bolognese Sauce
450g / 1lb / 2Cups Minced beef
1 sml Carrot finely chopped
1 Stick of celery finely chopped
1 Onion finely chopped
2 Cloves of garlic finely chopped
400g / 8oz / 1$^1/_2$Cups Tinned peeled tomatoes chopped with juice
1 Sprig of rosemary, one bay leaf tied together
60ml / 2floz / $^1/_4$Cup Olive oil
30 g/ 2Tb / 2T Butter
1 Glass Red wine
Bechamel sauce
30 g/ 2Tb / 2T Butter
30 g/ 2Tb / 2T Plain flour
500ml / 16floz / 2Cups Milk
5ml / 1tsp / 1t Mild mustard
Salt and pepper

CHEF'S TIP

When you cook bolognese sauce, tie kitchen twine around herbs and tie to handle of pot to aid removal.

Method

Make the béchamel sauce: melt the butter, add flour and cook for 1 min., add warm milk stirring constantly until it bubbles. Remove from heat, season with salt, pepper and add mustard.

Make Bolognese sauce: heat a heavy pot and add the olive oil, carrot, celery, onion and garlic. Cook over medium heat until softened for 5 mins.

Add the minced meat and cook until the meat has changed colour about 30 mins. Add wine, tomato and herbs. Bring to simmer over low heat. Stirring with a wooden spoon, continue cooking for one hour.

Before use, take out herbs and add butter for taste.

Preheat oven to 200^C/400^f/gas 6. Grease the ovenproof dish (preferably a rectangular shape) with butter. Pour some béchamel sauce in the bottom. Place the lasagne sheets on top. Place some bolognese sauce to cover lasagne sheets and then some béchamel sauce. Sprinkle some basil and parmesan.

Repeat with the lasagne sheets, bolognese sauce, béchamel sauce, basil and parmesan.

Lastly cover with the lasagne sheets. Pour over the béchamel sauce and a little bolognese sauce to cover. Sprinkle with the parmesan cheese and basil.

Place the slices of mozzarella cheese and a knob of butter on top.

Bake in oven for 25 mins.

Allow to rest for 15 mins before cutting.

Serve with one of our delicious salads and garlic bread.

Suggested Wine: Montepulciano d'Abruzzo

Beef Lasagne with Buffalo Mozzarella

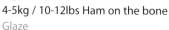

Christmas Ham

Serves 6

Ingredients

4-5kg / 10-12lbs Ham on the bone

Glaze

60g / 2oz / $\frac{1}{4}$Cup Brown sugar

45ml / 3Tb / 3T Mustard (wholegrain or plain)

45ml / 3Tb / 3T Honey

Whole cloves

Gluten free

CHEF'S TIP

If eating ham cold, cool completely in the cooking liquid before taking out and skinning.

Method

Put the ham into fresh cold water with an onion, carrot and a large bouquet garni. Pour in enough cold water to cover and bring to the boil. Reduce heat to simmer and skin off white froth which will form on top of water.

Simmer until cooked, allow 30 mins. for each 450g/1lb.

To Glaze

Strip off skin leaving the thick layer of fat. Score fat into diamond pattern.

Mix glaze mixture and cover skin surface.

Stud with cloves and sprinkles with brown sugar.

Bake in preheated oven 220^C/430^f/gas 8 for 20 mins., basting occasionally until skin is brown and crisp.

Suggested Wine: Beaujolais Cru-Morgon, Chiroubles, Moulin-a-Vent

Christmas Ham

Fish Dishes

Baked Fillet of Cod with Mango Salsa

Serves 4

Ingredients

4 x 175g / 6oz Fillets of fresh cod
25g / 1oz / $^1/_4$Cup Plain flour
1tb / 1T Sunflower oil

The Salsa

1 Ripe mango
4 Scallions
1 Red pepper, sliced and de-seeded
60ml / 2floz / 4T Olive oil
Salt and pepper
Juice of 1 lime
Pre heat oven to 180^c/350^f/gas 4

> **CHEF'S TIP**
>
> *If mangoes are not available use avocadoes or tomatoes and Coriander.*

Method

Make the salsa first as it can be made up to a day in advance. Peel and quarter the mango and remove the stone. Then slice it and cut it into small dice. Top, tail and wash the scallions and slice very finely down the length. Dice the pepper slices so that they are a small dice of about the same size as the mango pieces. Mix everything together in a bowl with the lime juice and season. Place in the fridge while cooking the fish.

Wipe down the fillets of cod with kitchen paper. Put the flour in a bowl or dish and dip the skin side of the fillets in the flour. Heat the oil in a pan and when good and hot, sear the cod in the pan, skin side down, for about 2 mins. Remove the fish from the pan (now the skin should be crispy) and put the fish in an ovenproof dish, skin side up this time. Bake in a preheated oven at 180^c/350^f/gas 4 for 7-10 mins., until fish is cooked through. When the fish is cooked serve it straight from the oven with a generous spoon of salsa on top.

 Nutritional Advice: Cod is low in fat, rich in vitamin B12, protein, iodine, sellenium, zinc and iron.

Suggested Wine: Macon Blanc-Vire, Clesse, or even from the best known village, Lugny.

Baked Fillet of Cod with Mango Salsa

Flaked Salmon over Spaghetti with Sun-dried Tomato and Rocket

Gluten free

Serves 4-6

Ingredients

325g / 12oz Cooked salmon fillet
75g / 3oz / $^1/_2$Cup Sun-dried tomatoes (keep the oil from the jar)
50g / 2oz / $^1/_2$Cup Rocket leaves
250g / 9oz Spaghetti
50g / 2oz $^1/_3$Cup Pinenuts

> **CHEF'S TIP**
>
> *For an added treat, you can use smoked salmon in place of the salmon fillet.*

Method

Since spaghetti varies, follow the instructions on the packet to cook. While the spaghetti is cooking toast the pine nuts under a moderate grill until lightly browned. Chop up the sun-dried tomatoes and place them, along with the oil, in a bowl. Add the pine nuts and the rocket. When the pasta is cooked drain it well and add it to the bowl and toss all the ingredients together. Before serving, flake the cold salmon fillet over the pasta. The hot and cold work very well together.

Suggested Wines: Mild Chardonnay from South Africa or Italy or Gerwurztraminer from Alsace or Chile.

Baked Cod Florentine with Cheddar and Mustard

Use the freshest of fish for this dish free from ice and water. This is a delicious, easy to prepare, lunch or supper dish.

Serves 6

Gluten free

Ingredients

1 Ovenproof dish, buttered
6 220g / 7oz Fillets of cod
2tb / 2T Wholegrain mustard
220g / 7oz / 2Cups Cheddar cheese, grated
260g / 8floz / 1Cup Cream
Sea salt and cracked pepper
200g / 8oz / 2Cups Prepared baby spinach

> **CHEF'S TIP**
>
> *Prepare all the ingredients and make up sauce in advance.*

Method

Pre-heat oven 200^C/400^f/gas 6
Trim and remove any bones from the fish. Set aside while you prepare the spinach.
Toss spinach in a little melted butter, season with salt and pepper. Place in the bottom of dish and arrange the fish on top.
In a bowl, mix together the cheese, cream and mustard. Pour over the fish.
Season with salt and pepper and sprinkle with paprika.
Bake in a preheated oven until golden on top (about 20-25mins.).
Serve immediately.

 Nutritional Advice: All varieties of seafood have great nutritional values with plenty of protein, minerals and vitamins. They are also low in fat

Suggested Wine: A good quality Pinot Gris, an unfairly maligned wine.

Flaked Salmon over Spaghetti with Sun-dried Tomato and Rocket

Fresh Salmon Fish Cakes with Celeriac Caper Salad

Celeriac is a great winter vegetable, wonderful in soups or roasted and makes a great potato mash.

Serves 6

Ingredients

450g / 1lb / 2Cups Fresh salmon, skinned and boned

350g /12oz / 2Cups Potatoes, peeled

50g / 2oz / 2T Butter

2 Eggs beaten

2 Leeks for garnish (white part only)

Lemons for garnish

125gr / 4oz / 1Cup Dried fresh breadcrumbs for coating

Sea salt and freshly ground pepper

Salad

Ingredients

1 Head Celeriac peeled and shredded

$1/_4$ Head White cabbage peeled and shredded

225g / 8oz / 2Cups Mangetout washed and trimmed

18 Capers rinsed

1 Bunch Fresh parsley chopped

$3/_4$Cup Mayonnaise

1 tsp / 1t Grated lemon rind

Salad

> ### CHEF'S TIP
> Prepare the Celeriac at the last minute to prevent discolouration.

Method

In a large bowl mix together the cabbage, celeriac, mangetout, lemon rind, parsley and capers. Add the mayonnaise to the ingredients and blend well to combine.

Leave for 1-2 hours for flavours to develop.

Fish cake

Method

Cook potatoes in boiling salted water.

When tender, drain and shake over heat until dry.

Mash or Sieve potatoes.

Steam or Poach Salmon for 15 mins.

When cool, flake and add to the potatoes.

Add butter and seasoning. To bind the mixture, add 1 beaten egg.

Divide into equal portions, shape and roll in flour. Dip in beaten egg and cover with the breadcrumbs.

Fry in hot pan until golden brown on both sides or deep fry.

Drain well and serve with frizzled leeks and wedges of lemon.

Garnish

Wash and thinly slice the leeks and dry well.

In a small heavy saucepan or deep-fat fryer, add leeks and fry until golden brown and frizzled.

Transfer to paper towels to drain.

Suggested Wine: Moderate White Burgundy- Macon, Rully, Montagny.

Fresh Salmon Fish Cakes with Celeriac Caper Salad

Kilkenny Fish Pie

Serves 6

Ingredients

1kg / 2lbs / 8Cups Peeled potatoes
450g / 1lb Cod
450g / 1lb Smoked haddock
855ml / $1^1/_2$pts / $3^3/_4$Cups Milk
150g / 6oz / $^3/_4$Cup Butter
3 Leeks thinly sliced
1tb / 1T Mustard
50g / 2oz / $^1/_2$Cup Plain flour
300ml / $^1/_2$pt / Dry cider or white wine
1tb / 1T Fresh parsley
2tb / 1T Lemon Juice
200g / 8oz / 2Cups Baby spinach
3 Hard boiled eggs
50g / 2oz / $^1/_2$Cup Chopped dill (reserve a little for garnish)
Salt and white pepper

Method

Put cod and haddock in large saucepan and cover with 700ml/$1^1/_4$pts/3Cups milk. Bring slowly to the boil. Simmer for 8-10 mins. until flesh is just cooked. Remove fish carefully and reserve milk.

In the meantime, cook potatoes until tender, drain well, mash or purée. Add 75g/3oz/6T of butter, salt and pepper to taste. Beat in 140ml/$^1/_4$pt/$^2/_3$Cup of warm milk.

Set aside and keep warm.

Preheat oven 190^C/375^F/gas 5.

Melt butter in large saucepan and add leeks. Cook gently for 5 mins. until soft, then add flour. Cook for 1 min, stir in cider or wine and then add reserved milk.

Add lemon juice, mustard and parsley. Season to taste. Set aside.

Flake the fish, removing skin and bones. Cut eggs into quarters, sauté spinach in a little butter until just wilted.

Put the fish in an ovenproof dish and add the spinach, eggs and dill..

Pour over the sauce.

Top with the mashed potato.

To glaze pie

Beat egg with 1tsp/1t water, using a pastry brush.

Brush egg wash evenly over potatoes and bake for 30 mins. until topping is crisp and golden. Garnish with fresh dill.

Nutritional Advice: All varieties of seafood have great nutritional values with plenty of protein, minerals and vitamins. They are rich in Iron, zinc and Iodine.

Suggested Wine: White Bordeaux.

Kilkenny Fish Pie

Seared Salmon with Kaffir Lime and Coconut Dressing on Rocket

Gluten free

When choosing fish, especially fillets, the flesh should look firm and spring back when lightly pressed. Seafood in a display counter should be well chilled. If on ice, the fish should not be in direct contact with the ice. For this dish we use the ends of a salmon.

Serves 6

Ingredients
Searing pan or grill.
24 strips of Salmon (4 strips each person)
A little oil
Sea salt and cracked pepper
200g / 8oz of Rocket

Dressing
4-6 Kafir lime leaves
2tb / 2T Lime juice and zest
2tb / 2T Coconut milk
1 Stick lemongrass, crushed
2 Limes for garnish

> **CHEF'S TIP**
> *Any firm fish would be suitable, particulary the ends of larger portions.*

Method

Combine dressing ingredients together and set aside.
To prepare salmon, cut into strips and dip in a little oil. Season with salt and pepper. Heat the grill or searing pan until hot. Cook fish for a few mins. on either side until golden. Wash and dry rocket, toss in dressing and arrange salmon on top.

 Nutritional Advice: *Exposed flesh in contact with melting ice will become soggy and soft and lose most of its nutritional value in the water. Salmon has anti-inflammatory properties.*

Suggested Wine: Australian Chardonnay.

Seared Salmon with Kaffir Lime and Coconut Dressing on Rocket

Gateaux of Smoked Salmon and Avocado

This dish is ideal as a starter or alternatively serve it with our delicious celeriac and caper salad (page 81) for a refreshing lunch.

Gluten free

Serves 4

Ingredients

3 Just ripening avocados
6 Tomatoes, quartered with seeds removed
5ml / 1tsp / 1t lemon juice
2 Small lemons or limes
500g / 1lb smoked salmon, sliced thinly
Black pepper and flat parsley

> **CHEF'S TIP**
>
> *Prepare the avocados last as even a short time in the air will cause them to go black, so they need to be added to the lemon juice very quickly.*

Method

You will need 10cm x 7cm/4in x 3in pastry cutters or cooking rings for this dish. Chop the de-seeded tomatoes into a fine dice. Peel and chop the avocado and mix with the tomato and the lemon juice. Place your rings in the centre of your serving plates and place a slice of smoked salmon in the base of your ring and press in. Then add a layer of the tomato and avocado. Then another layer of smoked salmon, and then another of tomato and avocado, topping off with a final layer of smoked salmon. Press the contents down well and repeat this process for all four rings. Then cover the rings with clingfilm and place them in the fridge for about 30 mins to set.

To serve, remove the ring, grind black pepper over the gateaux and garnish with half a lemon or lime and some flat parsley.

Gateaux of Smoked Salmon and Avocado

Poultry Dishes

Duck Breast with Oven-Roast Baby Potatoes

Gluten free

Serves 4

Ingredients
4 Duck breasts.
400g / 8oz / 2Cups Pitted black cherries
5floz / $^2/_3$Cups / $^1/_4$ Bottle dry red wine
25g / 1 oz / 1T Brown sugar
Drop of sunflower oil

Potatoes
450g / 1lb Baby potatoes
1tb / 1T Olive oil
4 Sprigs of rosemary
Sea salt and cracked pepper

> **CHEF'S TIP**
>
> *Duck fat is excellent for roasting potatoes, parsnips etc. so keep the fat from the duck breasts for use later.*

Method
Preheat the oven to 200^C/400^f/gas 6.

Put a tiny drop of sunflower oil in a frying pan and heat. Place breasts in the pan, skin side down and fry for 2-3 mins. until the skin starts to brown. Then turn the breast and fry on the skinless side.

After frying, place the breasts in an oven-proof dish on a roasting tray which will allow the duck fat to drain off. Put duck in oven for 20-30 mins. until each breast is solid when pressed with the back of a teaspoon.

When you have removed the duck from the oven, place on a warm dish and allow to rest for 10 mins. before serving.

Sauce
Place the entire contents of the can of cherries in a saucepan. Check through with a fork that there are no remaining stones. Using the fork, crush the cherries roughly, add the wine and bring to the boil. Simmer until the sauce reduces to half of its original volume. About half way through the simmering, taste the sauce. If it is slightly bitter, add a small amount of brown sugar, stir and continue to cook.

Place the sauce on serving plates and arrange duck breasts on top.

Potatoes
Warm the dish and the oil together in the oven for a minute. Add the potatoes and rosemary sprigs to the warm oil in the dish and stir them around to coat well. Now return the dish to the oven for about 30 mins. or until the potatoes are soft and golden.

Shake the flaked sea salt over the potatoes to serve.

Suggested Wine: Rioja Reserva.

Duck Breast with Oven-Roast Baby Potatoes

Breast of Chicken with Leek and Bacon Stuffing
and Grain Mustard Sauce

Serves 4

Ingredients
4 lrg Skinned and boned chicken breasts
1 med Leek
6 Rashers of back bacon
125g / 4oz / 2Cups Fresh breadcrumbs
15ml / 1tb / 1T Sunflower oil
Salt and pepper

> **CHEF'S TIP**
>
> *The chicken can be wrapped in cling film and steamed 20-25 minutes.*

Sauce
30ml /2 tb / 2T Grain mustard
60ml / 2floz / $^1/_4$Cup Cream
30ml / 2tb / 2T Vegetable or chicken stock

Method
Make the stuffing first (can be made the day before). Wash and clean the leek, then slice finely. Chop up the rashers also, and gently fry both together in the oil for about 3 mins. Then, when this mixture has cooled a bit, bind it together with the breadcrumbs and set aside. Wipe the chicken breasts with kitchen paper and open them out flat. Cut in under the mini fillet in the breast piece so as to make a pocket. Fill this pocket with the stuffing mix. Then roll up the chicken breast tightly to seal off the pocket and wrap it in a greased piece of tin foil, sealing the ends like a Christmas cracker. Place the wrapped breasts in an ovenproof dish with about 2.5cm/1in of water and bake in a preheated oven 200^C/400^f/gas 6 for 25-30 mins. Test by piercing the parcels and when it is cooked, it will run clear. While the chicken is cooking, make the mustard sauce by simply heating the stock with the mustard. When this mix comes to the boil, take it off the heat and allow it to cool slightly before adding the cream, so the cream does not separate. Keep the sauce warm on a very low simmer until serving.

Allow the chicken to rest for about 8 mins. before carving into slices. Drizzle the sauce over and serve with vegetables of your choice or one of our tempting salads.

Suggested Wine: Australian Shiraz Cabernet.

Breast of Chicken with Leek and Bacon Stuffing and Grain Mustard Sauce

Roast Corn-fed Chicken with Lemon and Rosemary

This simple but flavoursome dish is ideal for family gatherings on Sunday. The day before, marinade the chicken with the herbs, olive oil lemon zest and juice.

Serves 6-8

Gluten free

Ingredients

6-8 Chicken crowns or baby chicken (poussins)
Juice and zest of 3 Lemons
4 Garlic cloves
450g / 2lbs Shallots peeled
Bunch of fresh rosemary
6 Lemons, juice and lemon peel
Or
Preserved lemons (recipe follows)
6tb / 6T Olive oil
Sea salt and cracked pepper

> **CHEF'S TIP**
>
> *When using preserved lemons, use only the peel. Lime could be used for this recipe. Preserved lemons or limes are delicious with lamb or fish.*

Method

Prepare chicken for marinade: Wash and dry the chicken. In a large bowl big enough to hold chicken, add the juice of 3 lemons, whole garlic cloves and plenty of fresh rosemary, salt and pepper.
Leave overnight if you have time.
Preheat oven to 200c/400f/gas 6.
Peel shallots and add to the chicken and marinade. Toss and place chicken in a large roasting dish, crown side up.
Spoon over any remaining marinade.
Cook for one hour basting occasionally. After one hour add 3 preserved lemons (peel only), cut into eighths. If using fresh lemons, add them after 30 mins. of cooking time.
Continue cooking for 30 mins. more until the chickens are golden and cooked through.
Remove chicken pieces and cut in half.
Serve with the pan juices poured over.

Suggested Wine: Australian Chardonnay.

Preserved Lemons

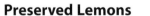

Ingredients
12 lemons
Sea salt

Method

Wash and cut incisions into each lemon so they are completely cut but held together at stem. Sprinkle in the salt and squeeze closed. Put into jars and sprinkle again with salt. Pour in boiling water to cover. After 3 weeks the liquid will be thick, salty and flavoured and ready for use.
Placed in sterilised jars they can be kept for 6 months.

Roast Corn-fed Chicken with Lemon and Rosemary

Chicken Tikka Masala

This dish has become popular all over the world. It is simple to cook and the choice of meat is a personal preference.

Serves 6

Ingredients

6 lrg Chicken breasts skinned
60ml / 4tb / 4T Lemon juice
5ml / 1tsp / 1t Salt
150g / 5oz / $^2/_3$Cup Single cream
275ml / $^1/_2$pt / 1$^1/_2$Cups Yogurt
250ml / 8floz / 1Cup Chicken stock
1tb / 1T Fresh grated ginger
1tb / 1T Fresh crushed garlic
3tsp / 3t Ground cumin
2tsp / 2t Ground coriander
2tsp / 2t Garam masala
2tsp / 2t Ground turmeric
1tsp / 1t Chilli powder
50g / 2oz / 4T Melted butter or oil
1 Red and 1 Green chilli chopped
1 Bunch fresh coriander to garnish
50g / 2oz Toasted almonds

Pilau Rice

275g / 10oz / 1$^1/_2$Cups Basmatic rice, washed and soaked for 30 mins.
75g / 3oz / $^1/_3$Cup Butter or oil
1 lrg Onion finely sliced
6 Green Cardamom pods split to release flavour
4 Cloves
13cm / 5in Pieces cassia bark or cinnamon stick halved
1tsp / 1t Ground Turmeric
$^1/_2$tsp / $^1/_2$t Salt
550ml / 18 floz / 2Cups Warm water

> **CHEF'S TIP**
>
> *If the sauce is too thick, add a little cream or stock before serving. Both rice and chicken can be prepared in advance.*

Method

Cut chicken into bite size pieces and place in a mixing bowl, add lemon juice and salt. Mix thoroughly and set aside for 30 mins. Mix the yoghurt and cream together and add to chicken mixture. Combine well, cover and leave to marinate in a cool place for 3 hours or overnight in the fridge. Heat butter in medium saucepan or wok. Add spices and cook for 5 mins., then add the chicken and cook for 5 mins. Add the marinade and a little stock, cook for a further 15-20 mins. While the chicken is cooking prepare rice.

Drain rice thoroughly, melt the oil or butter in a heavy saucepan over medium heat. Add onions and fry for 8 mins until browned reserve a little onion for garnish. Remove with slotted spoon, drain and set aside. Cook the Cardamom, cloves, and cassia bark for 20 secs.

Add rice, turmeric, salt and half of the fried onion.

Stir rice for a few minutes, add the water and bring to the boil. Boil for one minute and then reduce the heat to low.

Cover the pan tightly and cook for 10 mins. When the rice is ready, fork through and serve. Garnish with the remaining fried onion and sprigs of fresh coriander. Serve the chicken with rice and sprinkle the toasted almonds and coriander on top. Serve the diced chillies separately in a dish.

Suggested Wine: Rosè Tavel

Chicken Tikka Masala

New Year's Eve Duck

Ingredients
1 2kg / 4lbs Duck
1 Glass dry sherry
125g / 40oz / 2Cups Button mushrooms
30 ml / 2tsp / 2t Cooking oil
25g / 1oz / 2T Butter

Sauce
1tsp/1t Cooking oil
1tsp/1t Diced onion
1tsp/1t Diced carrot
1tsp/1t Diced celery
1tb / 1T Flour
600ml / 1pt / $2^1/_2$Cups Stock made from the bones of the duck.

Ingredients
Stuffing
1 Onion finely chopped
350g / 12ozs / $1^1/_2$Cups Pork or veal minced
125g / 4oz / $^3/_4$Cup Fresh breadcrumbs
15g /1tb / 1T Chopped parsley
1tsp / 1t Dry sage
1 Glass dry sherry
125g / 4oz / $^3/_4$Cup Ham cut into strips
10 Pistachio nuts blanched and peeled
1 Egg
275g / 10oz / $1^1/_4$Cups Butter
Salt and pepper

Method
Bone the duck or get your butcher to do it for you. Keep the bones for the stock. To make up stuffing.

Melt butter, sweat onions, cool and add to the minced meat and breadcrumbs. Mix with the herbs and sherry. Season well and bind with the beaten egg.

Open flesh of duck out on board – north to south. Spread the stuffing leaving a border.

Place the nuts down the centre in a line. Place the ham strips on either side of the nuts – on top of stuffing all going in the same direction.

Fold over ends and turn in sides. Roll up carefully like a sausage and sew it with a trussing needle. Then tie the duck tightly at 5cm/2in intervals.To cook, heat oil in roasting pan. Set duck on dish and baste with oil. Roast at 200^C/400^f/gas 6 and baste every 20 mins. After 40 mins. turn the duck over and cook for a further 30-40 mins. It should be crisp and golden in colour.

Stock
Cook the bones until well browned. Add 32floz / 2pts / 4Cups of water and simmer for 1-2 hours. Skim and strain before use. The stock can be prepared a day in advance.

Sauce
Cook diced onion, carrot and celery until golden in colour. Add 1tb / 1T of flour and cook for 1 min. Add stock and simmer until it thickens to a pouring consistency, strain and keep warm.

Prepare the mushrooms by slicing and cook in pan with butter until golden, set aside and keep warm.

When duck is cooked, remove and keep warm while you prepare the final stages of your brown sauce. Drain off excess fat from the roasting pan.

De-glaze pan with sherry. Add the drained stock and stir well, transfer to saucepan, add the mushrooms and keep warm.

Carve the duck diagonally into slices and serve with the sauce.

Suggested Wine: Chablis.

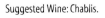

New Year's Eve Duck

Chicken and Broccoli Pie

Serves 6
Method

Preheat oven to 180ᶜ/350ᶠ/gas 4.
Cook potatoes until soft. Drain and mash, add salt, hot milk and half the butter. Beat until smooth. Keep warm.
Poach or steam chicken fillets until well cooked, reserving the stock for the sauce. Cool and cut into bite size pieces.
Steam broccoli until al dente, drain and refresh under cold water to preserve colour. Break into florets.
Make the sauce; melt the butter, add flour and cook for 1 min. Add warm stock stirring as it cooks and thickens. Season with salt and pepper, a pinch of nutmeg and mustard. Add the cream. The sauce should be of pouring consistency.
Pour sauce over chicken and broccoli and mix well.
Pipe potatoes on top. Beat egg with 1tsp/1t of water and brush over potatoes. Bake until bubbling and golden, about 25 mins.

Ingredients
5-6 Chicken fillets
8 Potatoes peeled
440g / 14oz / 3Cups broccoli
1Egg
30gr / 3tb 3T Flour
75gr / 3oz / 6T Butter
500ml / 1pt / 2Cups Chicken stock
150ml / 5oz / $^2/_3$Cup Milk
150ml / 5oz / $^5/_8$Cup Cream
Salt and pepper
2tsp / 2t Mustard
$^1/_2$tsp / $^1/_2$t Nutmeg

99

Chicken and Broccoli Pie

Bakery

Gluten-Free Orange Almond Cake

This cake is best eaten the day after it is baked, allow it to set for at least 24 hours before cutting.

Serves 8

Ingredients

2 Oranges
575ml / 1pt 2^1/$_2$Cups Water
450g / 16oz / 2^1/$_2$Cups Caster sugar
450g / 16oz / 4^1/$_2$Cups Ground almonds
6 Eggs
1 tsp / 1t Baking powder (gluten-free)
2tb / 2T Icing sugar

CHEF'S TIP

For a special occasion, add a measure (50ml/2floz) of Grand Marnier or Contreau to this cake.

Method

This cake requires a 25cm/10in round cake tin.
Pre-heat oven 200^C/400^f/gas 6.
Boil the oranges whole in the water for 15 mins. Allow the oranges to cool and cut in half and take out the seeds and liquidise with the remaining water until smooth. Whisk the eggs until light and fluffy and then add the sugar. Whisk for a further 5 mins. Add the almonds and baking powder and mix thoroughly. Add the orange mixture slowly and blend. Line the cake tin with parchment paper and add the cake mixture. Flatten out the surface. Bake for approximately 1^1/$_2$ hours. Lower the temperature to 180^C/350^f/gas 4 after 15 mins. Cool well before removing the tin. Dust with icing sugar.

Gluten-Free Pizza Base

Serves 8

Ingredients

225g / 8oz / Tritamyl flour (gluten-free)
75g / 3oz / ^{1}/$_3$Cup Margarine
1 Small egg
Pinch of Salt
30ml / 1tb / 1T Milk
Finely chopped basil

Method

Sieve the flour and salt together. Rub in margarine. Mix to a stiff dough with the egg, milk and basil.
Roll out dough to a quarter inch of thickness. Prick the top.
Spread tomato purée on top (to required taste).
Pile on the topping of your choice.
Finish off with grated cheese.
Bake in moderately hot oven 180^C/350^f/gas 4 for 35-40 mins.
It is not necessary to pre-heat oven as pizza will rise as oven heats.

Gluten Free Orange Almond Cake

American Style Baked Cheesecake

This is a delicious baked cheesecake rich in texture, colour and taste. A little goes a long way although it requires time and patience but the final result makes it worthwhile. You will need one round cake tin 20cm/8in well buttered.

As you bake this cake 'Bain-Marie' style to keep it moist, you will need one slightly larger Pan (for hot water) to place the cake tin on while baking.

Serves 6

Ingredients

1kg / 2lbs / 4Cups Cream cheese
4 lrg Eggs
2tb / 2T Biscuit crumbs
200g / 7oz / 1Cup Sugar
75g / 3oz Dark chocolate
2 Drops Almond-essence
3 Drops Vanilla-essence

CHEF'S TIP
This will keep for days in your fridge. Serve only small portions, no doubt there will be requests for second helpings.

Method

Preheat oven 180^C/350^f/gas 4.

Melt chocolate and set aside. In a mixer beat the cheese until smooth. Add vanilla and almond essence, add the sugar and beat again. Add the eggs one at a time, beat gently. Take two cups of the mixture and add the melted chocolate. Beat until smooth. Set aside.

Pour the light mixture into the prepared tin. Fill a pastry bag fitted with a plain nozzle 1$^1/_2$cm/$^1/_2$in and fill with chocolate mixture. Arrange cake tin at a comfortable level and pipe one large ball into the centre of the cake about 5cm/2in deep.

Adapt the same procedure and pipe 6 smaller dots around the cake, but do not let them touch each other. If you have some mixture left over, add it to the centre ball.

Place cake tin on a larger pan in the lowest part of the oven. Pour hot water in pan about 5cm/2in deep.

Bake for 1 hour until golden in colour. If you feel its browning too much, cover it with parchment paper. Top up water level as it evaporates quite quickly during the cooking process.

This cake will be firm on top but will be very moist and soft in the centre before refrigeration. Remove cake from the oven and leave to cool in the tin for 2 hours at room temperature. Have two large plates ready and carefully turn cake out and remove tin.

Sprinkle biscuit crumbs on bottom side and invert again into the other plate leaving the cake the right side up.

Refrigerate several hours or overnight.

Suggested Wine: Lightish sweet white. Vouvay or Orvieto Amabile - possibly Coteaux de Layon which is heavier.

American Style Baked Cheesecake

Apple Cake

Serves 6

Ingredients

30ml / 2tb / 2T Brandy
75g / 3oz / $^1/_2$Cup Currants or sultanas
250g / 9oz / 1$^1/_2$Cups Self raising flour
125g / 5oz / $^5/_8$Cup Butter
125g / 5oz / $^2/_3$Cup Caster sugar
1tsp / 1t Ground ginger
1tsp / 1t Ground cinnamon
450g / 1 lb / 4 med Granny Smith apples
2 Beaten eggs
Icing sugar to decorate

> **CHEF'S TIP**
>
> Pears can replace apples for this cake.

Method

Butter the sides and base of a 18cm/7in drop bottomed cake tin and dust lightly with flour. Place the brandy and dried fruit in a bowl to soak. Sift the flour into another bowl and rub in the butter (until the mixture is like fine crumbs). Add the ginger, sugar and cinnamon. Peel the apples, quarter and remove the core. Then chop the quarters into small chunks into the flour mix. Add the soaked fruit and egg to the flour and mix thoroughly. Spoon the mixture into the tin and smooth the top flat. Bake for 25-35 mins. in a pre-heated oven 180^C/350^f/gas4.
To test the cake is fully baked, pierce with a skewer and if it comes out clean and dry, the cake is baked. If there are signs of dough on the skewer, put the cake back in the oven for a few more minutes.
Once baked, the cake needs at least 10 mins. cooling time before it is taken out of the tin.
Serve while still warm with ice cream for dessert, or on its own for afternoon tea.

Suggested Wine: Lightish sweet white. Vouvay or Orvieto Amabile - possibly Coteaux de Layon which is heavier.

Apple Cake

Savoury Pinwheels

Serves 6

Ingredients

1 Pack ready rolled puff pastry
25g / 1oz / 1T Grated parmesan
15ml / 1tb / 1T Black olive paste

Method

Spread out the sheet of puff pastry and cut in half (having thawed it if necessary). Spread one half with the black olive paste and the other with the grated parmesan. Then, very carefully, roll up the pastry sheet tightly taking care to seal the join along the length. At this stage, the pastry roll should look like a sausage with a spiral of the filling visible at each end.

Wrap the 2 rolls in cling film and place it in the fridge for at least an hour. When you are ready to bake the savouries, heat the over to 190^C/375^f/gas 5 and lightly grease a baking sheet. Take the rolls of pastry and slice them up into wheels about 2.5cm/1in thick and place on the baking tray spaced well apart to allow for raising. Bake in the oven for approximately 6 to 8 mins or until golden brown.

Serve immediately.

Butter Cookies

Serves 6

Ingredients

225g / 8oz / 2Cups Self-raising flour
225g / 8oz / 1Cup Butter
100g / 4oz / $^1/_2$Cup Caster sugar
5ml / 1tsp / 1tb Vanilla essence
50g / 2oz / $^1/_3$Cup Raisins

Method

Cream the butter and sugar together in a mixer (using a paddle beater, not a whisk) until it loses the graininess and becomes pale. Add the raisins and vanilla essence then fold in the sifted flour slowly. Once the flour is blended in, knead the mixture to smooth it out and place in the fridge for 30mins. to set.

To bake, heat the oven to 180^C/350^f/gas 4. Dust your work surfaces with flour and roll out the cookie dough to about 3cm/1in thickness. Use 5cm/2in cookie cutter to cut out, and then place the cookies onto a greased baking tray and into the oven for approx 10 mins. or until golden brown.

When baked, place on a wire rack tray to cool. If kept in an airtight container, these cookies will keep well for up to 5 days.

Butter Cookies

Savoury Pinwheels

Fruit Soda bread

Ingredients
200ml / 9floz / 1Cup Milk
225g / 8oz / 1Cup Mixed dried fruit
225g / 8oz / $1^{1}/_{2}$Cups Brown sugar
450g / 16oz / $4^{1}/_{2}$Cups Self raising flour
1 tsp / 1t Mixed spice

> **CHEF'S TIP**
>
> *Parchment paper is grease proof paper that has already been greased* and is ideal for baking or general cooking as it enables you to lift off food without sticking or baking.

Method

Combine all the dry ingredients together and then add the milk and mix again thoroughly. Line a loaf tin with parchment paper and spoon in the mixture, smoothing out the top. Place the loaf in a preheated oven at $180^{C}/350^{f}$/gas 4 for 1 hour. Cool in the tin for at least 10 mins. before moving to a wire tray to cool fully.

White Soda Bread

Ingredients
450g / 16oz / $4^{1}/_{2}$Cups Plain flour
$^{1}/_{4}$tsp / $^{1}/_{4}$t Salt
1 tsp / 1t Bread soda
1tb / 1T Sugar
250ml / 8floz / 1Cup Buttermilk or fresh milk
Method
Pre-heat oven $180^{C}/350^{f}$/gas 4.
Sieve the flour, breadsoda and salt into a large bowl and mix with the sugar. Make a well in the centre and add the milk. Stir all the ingredients together until it forms a pliable dough. Dust the work surface with flour, turn the dough out and gently knead it until it becomes smooth and elastic. Flatten it out into a circle about 2.5cm/1in thick. Place the bread on a greased and floured baking tray. Cut a cross into the surface to about half its depth and bake for 30-40 mins. until golden brown.

Tea Brack

Ingredients
400ml / 14floz / $1^{3}/_{4}$Cups Cold tea
200g / 7oz / 1Cup Brown sugar
350g / 12oz Fruit mix
275g / 10oz / $2^{3}/_{4}$Cups Self raising flour
1 Egg
Method
Put the tea, sugar and fruit mix into a bowl, cover and leave overnight. Add the egg and flour and mix well. Bake in a lined tin for $1^{1}/_{2}$-2 hours at $180^{C}/350^{f}$/gas 4.

110

Fruit Soda Bread

White Soda Bread

Apple Tart

This apple tart is very popular in Kilkenny with numerous requests for the recipe.

Serves 6

Ingredients

225g / 8oz / 2Cups Plain flour
75g / 3oz / $^1/_3$Cup Butter diced
75g / 3oz / $^1/_3$Cup Lard diced
100ml / 3floz / $^1/_3$Cup Ice cold water
Pinch of salt
30g / 2tb / 2T Granulated sugar
6-8 Cooking apples or Granny Smith apples
$^1/_4$tsp Ginger
$^1/_4$tsp Cinnamon
1 pie dish 23cm / 9in Wide
1 Egg for glazing

> ### CHEF'S TIP
> *The secret of tender tart pastry is to add as little water as possible and to handle the mixture gently and quickly.*

Method

Pre-heat oven to 200^c/400^f/gas 6.

Firstly prepare the pastry: combine sieved flour and salt in bowl. Cut butter and lard into flour until it resembles firm breadcrumbs. Add enough iced water to make a pliable dough.
Turn out on to a floured surface and knead until smooth. Divide in half, wrap and chill for 30 mins.
Peel, core and slice apples and toss in bowl with cinnamon, ginger and sugar.
Roll out the pastry about 30cm/12in wide into 2 circles. Lay one circle on pie dish, arrange apples on top. Brush edges with the water to seal. Cover with second round and press edges together to trim any excess pastry and crimp edges. Make 3 slits to allow steam to escape.
Brush with egg wash and bake for 30 mins. in the centre of the oven.

Suggested Wine: A sweetish white or fruity German wine. Avoid anything marked Trocken but below the rank of Kabinett.

Apple Tart

Orange Butter Scones

Serves 6

Ingredients

450g / 16oz / 4Cups Plain flour
3tsp / 3t Baking powder
50g / 2oz / $^1/_4$Cup Granulated sugar
85g / 3oz / 6T Butter
2 Eggs
230ml / 8floz / 1Cup Milk
Zest of 1 Orange
2 Drops of orange scented oil

Orange Butter Scones

Filling ingredients

Zest of 2 Oranges and juice
85g / 3oz / 6T Butter
125g / 4oz / $^3/_4$Cup Icing sugar

Method
Preheat oven to 200^C/400^f/gas 6.
Butter the baking tray.
Makes about 14-16 scones.

CHEF'S TIP
To enjoy these delicious scones at their best, eat while still warm.

Firstly prepare the filling.
Beat butter, zest of oranges and icing sugar together until smooth and creamy. Now prepare your scone mixture. In a large bowl, sieve flour, baking powder and add in sugar. Then add butter into dry ingredients until it resembles breadcrumbs. Add zest and oil.
Make a well in centre and add eggs, milk and orange juice. Mix together to make a soft dough.
Turn out on to a floured board and roll to a square. Spread the butter filling over and roll up like a swiss roll. Cut evenly into 14-16 slices and place on a buttered baking dish, circle side up leaving room between each scone as they will expand during cooking.
Bake in the oven for 16 mins.

Asian Fruit dipped in Chocolate

Ingredients
225g / 8oz Dark chocolate
225g / 8oz White chocolate
You can use a variety of dried fruit. Here are a few suggestions:
Dried mango slices
Dries papaya slices
Dried pineapple slices
Dried coconut slices
Fresh strawberries

Serve as a snack or after dinner with coffee. They make an unusual presentation for the Christmas table.
Method
Melt the chocolate in two separate bowls. Dip to coat half way, allow to dry before serving.

CHEF'S TIP
Dried fruits may be prepared in advance, however, the fresh strawberries should be dipped on the day as they go soggy.

Suggested Wine: Australian Muscats. Available in $^1/_2$ Bottles.

Plum Pudding

This recipe makes 5 x 1lb puddings or 2 x 2$^1/_2$lbs puddings

225g / 8oz / 2Cups Self-raising flour
2tsp / 2t Ground mixed spice
1tsp / 1t salt
450g / 16oz / 2Cups Butter
225g / 8oz / 4Cups Fresh white breadcrumbs
450g / 16oz / 3Cups Dark soft brown sugar
450g / 16oz / 3Cups Seedless raisins
450g / 16oz / 3Cups Sultanas
450g / 16oz / 3Cups Currants
100g / 4oz / $^1/_2$Cup Mixed candied peel chopped
100g / 4oz / $^1/_2$Cup Glace cherries chopped
2 med Carrots peeled or grated
6 Eggs beaten
125ml / 4floz / $^1/_2$Cup Brandy or Irish stout
2tb / 2T Black treacle
Finely grated rind and juice of 1 orange
Finely grated rind and juice of 1 lemon

CHEF'S TIP

Make this pudding at least four weeks before christmas.

Plum Pudding

Method

Sift the flour with mixed spice and salt. Stir in the soft butter, breadcrumbs and sugar. Add the dried fruit, candied peel, cherries and carrots. Stir well.

Add the beaten eggs, brandy or stout, black treacle and then add the orange and lemon rind and their juice. Mix until thoroughly combined and leave for three or four hours, stirring occasionally to let the flavour develop (and don't forget to make a wish!)

Preferably leave covered to stand overnight.

Spoon mixture into buttered bowls, pressing it down well. Leave room at top of bowl to let pudding rise. Cover with two circles of buttered greaseproof paper and then cover again with tin foil and tie securely with twine. Make sure that they are well and tightly covered.

Place the puddings in a pot with gently bubbling hot water. Cover with a lid and then gently boil for about 7-8 hours. Make sure you keep topping up the water level as necessary. The water must reach $^2/_3$ up the side of the bowl. Remove all the paper and when cold, cover with fresh greaseproof paper and a fitted lid or tin foil.

Store in a cool dry place.

To serve:

Steam for 3 hours before serving. Bring the pudding to the table and pour brandy over and light immediately. Serve with brandy butter and cream. Delicious!

Suggested Wine: South African late-harvest Riesling.

Christmas Cake

Ingredients

You will need a 25cm/10in cake tin

450g / 16oz / 3C. Sultanas
450g / 16oz / 3C. Raisins
225g / 8oz / 1^2/$_3$C. Currants
225g / 8oz / 1^1/$_2$C. Mixed peel
125g / 4oz / 1^1/$_4$C. Ground almonds
125g / 4oz / ^{3}/$_4$C. Almonds split
125g / 4oz / 1C. Apricots dried
125g / 4oz / ^{3}/$_4$C. Glace cherries
5tb / 5T of Brandy or Whiskey
450g / 16oz / 4C. Flour
1/5g / 6oz / ^{3}/$_4$C. Caster sugar
175g / 6oz / 1C. Brown sugar
350g / 12oz / 1^1/$_2$C. Butter
1 Orange, juice and zest
1 Lemon, juice and zest
6 lrg eggs
1tsp / 1t Mace
1tsp / 1t Nutmeg
1tsp / 1t All spice
(Sieve these three spices
with the flour)

Make sure that you have the correct cake tin, parchment paper and brown paper.
Ensure all your spices, flour and sugar are fresh. Start preparing your ingredients and cake tin a day in advance of baking.

Method

The day before

Prepare the fruit: Chop the apricots, almonds, cherries and peel. Mix all the fruit, apricots, almonds, cherries and peel together in a large bowl or basin. Cover and leave at room temperature overnight.
Prepare your cake tin by lining the insides, bottom and sides with parchment paper (3 layers in all) allowing paper to extend 5cm/2in over the cake tin. Finely fold a double layer of brown paper around the outside and secure with string.

The following Day

Preheat the oven to 160^C/330^f/gas3.
Cream butter and sugar until light. Add the beaten eggs one at a time with 2tsp/2t of flour. Repeat until eggs are incorporated. Do not over beat the mixture.
Fold the remaining flour gently with the spices and ground almonds. Add the fruit and nut mixture and fold in. Now add the spirits, the juices and zest of the orange and lemon, making sure that they are well blended. Pour into prepared tin and smooth over the top.
Place on middle shelf and bake.
After 35 mins., cover the top of cake with parchment paper and reduce heat to 140^C/275^f/gas1 . Bake for a further 4 hours. Test with a skewer before taking the cake out.
Reduce heat further if cake is over-browning.
Leave to cool in tin.
Remove and peel off paper.
 Wrap well until you are ready to decorate with icing.

Suggested Wine: Lightishish fruity Ruby Port, or Bual from Madeira

Christmas Cake

Plum Pudding

Orange Butter Scones

Asian Fruit Dipped in Chocolate

Gluten-Free Scones

Makes about 14 scones

Ingredients

450g / 16 oz / 4Cups Gluten-free flour

50g / 2oz / $^{1}/_{4}$Cup Granulated sugar

75g / 3oz / $^{1}/_{3}$Cup Butter

250ml / 8floz / 1Cup Milk

3 Eggs and 1 Egg for glazing

Method

Preheat oven to 200^{c}/400^{f}/gas 6

CHEF'S TIP

Why not double the quantites and freeze half for later use.

In a large bowl, mix all dry ingredients together. Add eggs and milk and combine well.

Turn out on to a floured board and knead gently to form a smooth pliable dough.

Roll out to about 2.5cm/1in in height. Flour a scone cutter and gently cut out your scones. Place on baking tray.

Egg wash and bake.

Bake in oven for 15-20 mins.

Gluten-Free Scones

Desserts

Sticky Toffee Pudding with Toffee Sauce

Serves 6

Ingredients
175g / 6oz / 1Cup Prunes or dates
200ml / 7oz / $^3/_4$Cup Water
1tsp / 1t Bicarbonate of soda
50g / 2oz / $^1/_4$Cup Butter
175g / 6oz / $^3/_4$Cup Caster sugar
2 Eggs beaten
175g/ 6oz / 1$^1/_2$Cups Self raising flour
1 tsp / 1t Vanilla essence

The sauce
300ml / 8floz / 1$^1/_4$Cups Cream
50g / 2oz / $^1/_4$Cup Demerara sugar
2tsp / 2t Black treacle

> **CHEF'S TIP**
>
> *This pudding can be served with custard, ice cream or fresh cream.*

Method
You will need a 25cm/10in sq baking tin, lined with parchment paper.
Pre-heat the oven to 180^C/350^f/gas 4.
Boil dates or prunes in the water for 5 mins. Add the bicarbonate of soda and keep the fruit in the water. Cream together the butter and sugar until light and fluffy then add the eggs and beat well. Add the flour and fold in. Mix in the fruit and water then pour the mixture into the baking tin. Bake for 35-40 mins., until just firm to the touch.
While the pudding is cooking, prepare the sauce.
Blend the ingredients together in a saucepan over a low heat stirring until the sauce comes too the boil, remove from the heat and set aside. Cut the pudding into portions and pour on the sauce.
Serve immediately.

Sticky Toffee Pudding with Toffee Sauce

Fresh Fruit Salad

An excellent variety of fresh fruits are available year round, as well as imported exotic fruits. This fruit salad is delicious for breakfast, lunch or dessert. It is great with yoghurt, crème fraîche or fresh cream.

Serves 6

Ingredients

CHEF'S TIP

A dash of cointreau will liven up any fruit salad.

1 Pineapple
2 Red apples
2 Oranges
1 Melon of your choice
175g / 6oz / 1Cup Black or green seedless grapes
125g / 4oz / $^3/_4$Cup Strawberries or mixed berries
Lemon juice

Method

Prepare pineapple. Remove skin, core and cut into bite size pieces. Peel core and cut apples into chunks, sprinkle with lemon juice to prevent discolouration.
Peel oranges and cut in slices. Peel melon, remove seeds and cut into bite size pieces. Wash grapes and strawberries and check over. Combine all the fruit together. Decorate with a sprig of mint or thyme.

 Nutritional Advice: Experts recommend that we eat at least five servings of fruit a day.

Mont Blanc Meringues

Serves 6

Gluten free

Ingredients
350g / 12oz / 1Cup Sweet chestnut purée
6 Meringue nests
600ml / 20floz / $2^1/_2$Cups Cream
2tsp / 2t Icing sugar
Method
Fill each meringue nest with 50g/2oz of the chestnut purée.
Whip the cream and swirl on top to form small peaks.
Dust with icing sugar.

Fresh Fruit Salad

Dried Fruit Salad

Many different dried fruits are available from supermarkets and health food shops. They can be eaten as a snack, added to cereals or used in puddings and pies.

Serves 6-8

Ingredients

450g / 16oz / 3Cups Dried fruit.
You can use any combination of the following:

Pineapples
Apricots
Apple rings
Figs
Prunes
Banana chips

1Cinnamon stick
500ml / 16floz / 2Cups Orange juice
1tsp / 1t Mixed spices

Method

Check fruit well before soaking.
Soak fruits overnight in prepared syrup of orange juice, mixed spices and cinnamon stick.
Next morning your dried fruit will be lovely and plump and ready to eat.
This will keep well for 5-7 days in the fridge, so you could double the above amount.

Nutritional Advice: Dried fruits are an excellent nutritionious food as they are high in fibre, rich in energy, protein, iron, calcium and vitamins A and B. Cinnamon has antiseptic properties and is good for settling an upset stomach.

Dried Fruit Salad

Honey-Baked Nectarines with Crème Fraîche

Gluten free

Serves 6

Ingredients
6 Nectarines (not too ripe)
90ml / 6tb / 6T Honey
90ml / 6tb / 6T Water
225g / 8oz / 1Cup Crème fraîche

CHEF'S TIP
Peaches can be used instead of nectarines.

Method
Wash the nectarines and pat them dry with kitchen paper. Cut each nectarine in half and remove the stone. Place the halves in an oven proof dish and drizzle the honey over each one. Add the water to the dish and bake in the oven at 180^C/350^f/gas 6 for 10-12 mins., until fruit has softened. Remove from dish and place on serving plates with the crème fraîche and mint.

Cappuccino Cup of Tiramisu

Serves 4

Ingredients
60ml / 2oz / 4T Amaretto liqueur
450g / 16oz / 2Cups Mascarpone cheese
50g / 2oz / $^1/_4$Cup Caster sugar
2tb / 2T Cream
300ml /10oz / 1$^1/_4$Cups Cold strong coffee
12-16 Boudoir biscuits halved
25g / 1oz / 2T Cocoa powder to garnish

CHEF'S TIP
You can substitute any liqueur of your choice.

Method
Add half your liquor to the coffee in a bowl. Now whip the mascarpone, the remaining liquor, the sugar and the cream together until well blended and smooth. Dip the boudoir biscuits for a moment in the coffee mix. Place the biscuits in the coffee cups and cover with the mascarpone until the cups are full to the brim. Smooth over the top surface and place the cups in the fridge for about 1 hour before serving.
To serve, sprinkle cocoa powder over the cups and then place on a saucer with a teaspoon.

Suggested Wine: Muscat de Beaumes de Venise. Available in $^1/_2$ Bottles.

Honey - Baked Nectarines with Crème Fraîche

Cappuccino Cup of Tiramisu

Terrine of Champagne and Strawberries

This dessert is a wonderful treat for any festive occassion.

Serves 4-6

Ingredients

450g / 16oz / 2$^1/_2$Cups Strawberries
1 Bottle Champagne
125g / 4 oz / $^1/_2$Cup Caster sugar
12 Leaves of gelatine
150ml / 4floz / $^2/_3$ Cup Water

Method

Soak the gelatine with the water in a saucepan, until it begins to go jelly-like, for about 5 mins. Heat this mixture over a moderate flame and stir until all the gelatine is dissolved. Add the sugar and dissolve. Now, take the mixture off the heat and add the champagne and whisk it together. This will froth, but this is normal and it will settle down when the mixture is left aside for a few minutes.
Wash and hull the strawberries.
Cut the strawberries into quarters and fill your glasses to about 2.5cm/1in from the top. Add the champagne to the glass.
When the glasses are completely cold, stand them in the fridge for 1 hour to set.

Terrine of Champagne and Strawberries

Kilkenny Ultimate Trifle

Allow time to prepare this dish so flavours can mature.

Serves 6

Ingredients

10 Trifle sponge fingers, madeira cake or genoise sponge
200g / 7 oz / $^3/_4$Cup Blackberry jam
400g / 14oz / 4Cups Blackberries
400g / 14oz / 3Cups Raspberries
1 Carton of ready made custard
800g / 32oz / 4Cups Mascarpone cheese
50g / 2oz / $^1/_2$Cup Flaked almonds toasted
50g / 2oz / $^1/_2$Cup Amaretti biscuits crushed
1 Wineglass of Amaretti liqueur or sherry, rum or brandy.

> **CHEF'S TIP**
>
> *Any sweet biscuits can be used in this recipe.*

Method

Prepare raspberries and blackberries and set aside. Toast almonds and split sponge in half and spread with a little of the jam and sandwich together. Warm jam very slightly, adding raspberries and blackberries. Stir very gently, reserving a quarter of the berries to line the base of the bowl.

To combine trifle

Scatter berries at base, arrange sponge fingers on top. Pour over Amaretti liqueur, then the jam and berries mixed. Let it drizzle through.
Add the custard to the mascarpone cheese and blend until smooth. Place on top of the jams and berries. Leave to mature in the fridge for at least 4 hours or overnight.
Decorate with flaked almonds and crushed biscuits and serve.

Suggested Wine: Sautenes.

Kilkenny Ultimate Trifle

Suggested Menus

When planning a menu you should balance your meals with a variety of flavours to satisfy the palate. Considering textures, colours and flavours, keeping in mind the seasons when the freshest ingredients are available.

Before starting to cook from a recipe, the first step should be to read the entire recipe to avoid any hidden surprises. Some recipes require you to plan in advance.

Check your portions depending on how many people you are cooking for and calculate accordingly.

Finally, when entertaining never try a dish for the first time.

Spring

Seared Salmon with Kaffir Lime and Coconut Dressing -pg85

Roast Corn-fed Chicken with Lemon and Rosemary -pg.93

Potato Nicoise -pg.61

Tomato & Zucchini Bake -pg.63

Fresh Fruit Salad -pg.121

Suggested Wine: Australian Chardonnay or South African Riesling.

Summer

Watermelon, Feta & Watercress Salad -pg.37

Baked Fillet of Cod with Mango Salsa -pg.77

Roast Tikka Potatoes -pg.61

Honey Baked Nectarines with

Crème Fraîche -pg.125

Suggested Wine: Macon Lugny or Tokay.

Autumn

Pumpkin & Sweetcorn Chowder -pg.27

Braised Beef Casserole with Irish Stout -pg.71

Aloo Chat -pg.61

Kilkenny Ultimate Trifle -pg.129

Suggested Wine: Red Bordeaux and Sauternes.

Winter

Creamy Asparagus Soup -pg.21

New Year's Eve Duck -pg.97

Broccoli Purée with Parmesan and Nutmeg -pg.55

Terrine of Champagne and

Strawberries -pg.127

Suggested Wine: Chablis or Champagne.

Vegetarian

Crisp Carrot and Zucchini with Thyme Vinaigrette -pg.36

Cherry Tomato, Artichoke and Gruyérè Cheese Frittata -pg.55

Tabbouleh -pg.51

Escalavida -pg.59

American Style Baked

Cheesecake -pg.103

Suggested Wine: Light fruity German or Austrian.

KILKENNY

European and American Culinary terms

EUROPEAN	AMERICAN
Apples-Cooking	Green Apples
Aubergine	Eggplant
Beans-French or green	Snap beans
Beetroot	Beet
Biscuit	Cookie
Broad bean	Fava bean
Butter beans	Lima beans
Cake tin	Cake pan
Caster sugar	Superfine granulated
Chickpeas	Garbanzo beans
Cider	Apple cider
Cling film	Plastic wrap
Corn flour	Corn starch
Courgette	Zucchini
Coriander	Cilantro
Crystallised fruits	Candied fruits
Double cream	Heavy cream
Dripping	Fat from roast
Flour-Plain	All purpose flour
Fresh	Raw
Gammon	Ham
Glace cherries	Candied cherries
Greaseproof paper	Waxed paper
Grill	Skillet
Grilling	Broiling
Icing sugar	Confectioners sugar
Joint of meat	Roast
Kitchen paper	Kitchen towel
Loaf tin	Loaf pan
Mince	Ground meat
Mustard-French	Prepared mustard
Mustard-English	Dry mustard
Pie dish	Deep baking dish
Pips	Seeds
Potatoes-Creamed	Mashed potatoes
Pudding	Dessert
Purée	Paste
Prawns	Shrimps
Soya sauce	Soy sauce
Stalk	Stem
Starter	Appetizer
Sticks-Celery	Stalks
Stock	Broth
Sultanas	Golden raisins
Sweetcorn	Corn
Swiss roll	Jelly roll
Treacle	Molasses
Vanilla essence	Vanilla extract
Whip or whisk	Beat

Glossary of Terms

Al Dente. Literally meaning "to the tooth". The texture of the food must have a bite to it.
Amaretto. An apricot liqueur.
Balsamic Vinegar. From Modena in Italy, which has been aged slowly in oak casks.
Baste. To spoon melted butter, fat or liquid over foods.
Bay leaves. Used to season food such as beef, pork, veal or chicken.
Blanch. To plunge food into boiling water and then boil it until it has softened or wilted.
Blend. To mix foods together less vigorously than beating.
Bouquet Garni. A bouquet consists of bayleaf, a sprig of thyme and four parsley stalks.
Braise. To brown food in fat, then cook in a covered casserole.
Bulghar wheat. Used in Middle Eastern dishes, it is wheat, hulled and crushed.
Capers. The grey-green bud of a warm climate used to enhance dressings.
They can be bought salted or pickled.
Celeriac. Root vegetable, darkish skin with white flesh.
Chickpeas. Known also as garbanzos – a round straw coloured dried legume.
Coconut cream. Made from coconut flesh and water.
Coeliac. An intolerance to wheat.
Couscous. Made from semolina, it is fine or course in texture.
Créme fraîche. A thick cream which is partially soured. It is less rich then fresh cream.
Croûtes. A round of bread fried or toasted or browned in the oven.
Croûtons. Small cubes of stale bread fried or slowly cooked in an oven.
De-glaze. Adding liquid to a pan in which foods have been sautéed or roasted, in order to dissolve the coagulated juices left in the pan. The basis for many sauces and gravies
De-grease. To pour off or skim with a spoon any surplus fat from a liquid or a pan.
Dice. To cut food into cubes, the shape of a dice.
Egg- wash. Beaten egg brushed over raw pastry, potato or scones to give them a shiny glaze when cooked.
Fish sauce. Also known as nam pla. Made from salted fermented fish.
Fold. To blend a fragile mixture.
Gratine. To brown the top of a sauced dish.
Gluten-free. Produce free of wheat.
Hull. To prepare strawberries, remove the green hull.
Julienne. The size and shape in which vegetables or garnishes should be cut.
It is the length of a matchstick.
Kaffir Lime leaves. They are the leaves of a citrus tree. Used fresh or dried in salads and many Asian dishes.
Lemon Grass. A lemon scented tall grass. Use only the white part for cooking.
Liaison. An element used for the binding together of a sauce or soup.
Marinate. To soak meat, fish or poultry with wine, oil, herbs or yoghurt to flavour before cooking.
Marsala. A sweet dry fortified wine from Italy.
Mixed spices. A blend of ground sweet spices, ie. cinnamon, cloves, nutmeg and ginger.
Noodles. Cellophane made from green mung bean flour. Good for soups or deep fried.
Palette Knife. A knife with a rounded tip and a flexible blade for spreading jam or cream etc.
Poach. Food submerged and cooked in a liquid that is barely simmering.
Purée. To render solid food into a mash such as mashed potatoes or vegetables.
Reduce. To boil down a liquid while the lid is off the saucepan.
Refresh. To pour cold water over vegetables to set the colour and prevent further cooking.
Rocket. A peppery salad leaf.
Soy sauce. Made from fermented soy bean.
Sweat. To cook vegetables with the lid on, on low heat in butter or oil until they are soft but not coloured .
Tritamyl flour. Gluten-free flour.
Vermouth. A flavoured white wine made from herbs and flavourings.
Zest. The thin coloured skin of an orange or lemon.
Zucchini. Known also as courgette.

Index